THE WORST DAY

THE WORST DAY

*A Plane Crash, A Train Wreck, and
Remarkable Acts of Heroism
in Washington, DC*

Bruce Goldfarb

STEERFORTH PRESS
LEBANON, NEW HAMPSHIRE

For information about permission to reproduce
selections from this book, write to:
Steerforth Press, 31 Hanover Street, Suite 1
Lebanon, New Hampshire 03766

Cataloging-in-Publication Data is available from the Library of Congress

ISBN 978-1-58642-416-9

Printed in the United States of America

EU RP (for authorities only): eucomply OÜ, Pärnu mnt. 139b-14, 11317,
Tallinn, Estonia, hello@eucompliancepartner.com, +33757690241

1 3 5 7 9 10 8 6 4 2

Other Books by Bruce Goldfarb

*18 Tiny Deaths: The Untold Story of Frances Glessner
Lee and the Invention of Modern Forensics*

OCME: Life in America's Top Forensic Medical Center

*Dedicated to first responders
and every person who steps up
to act when it matters*

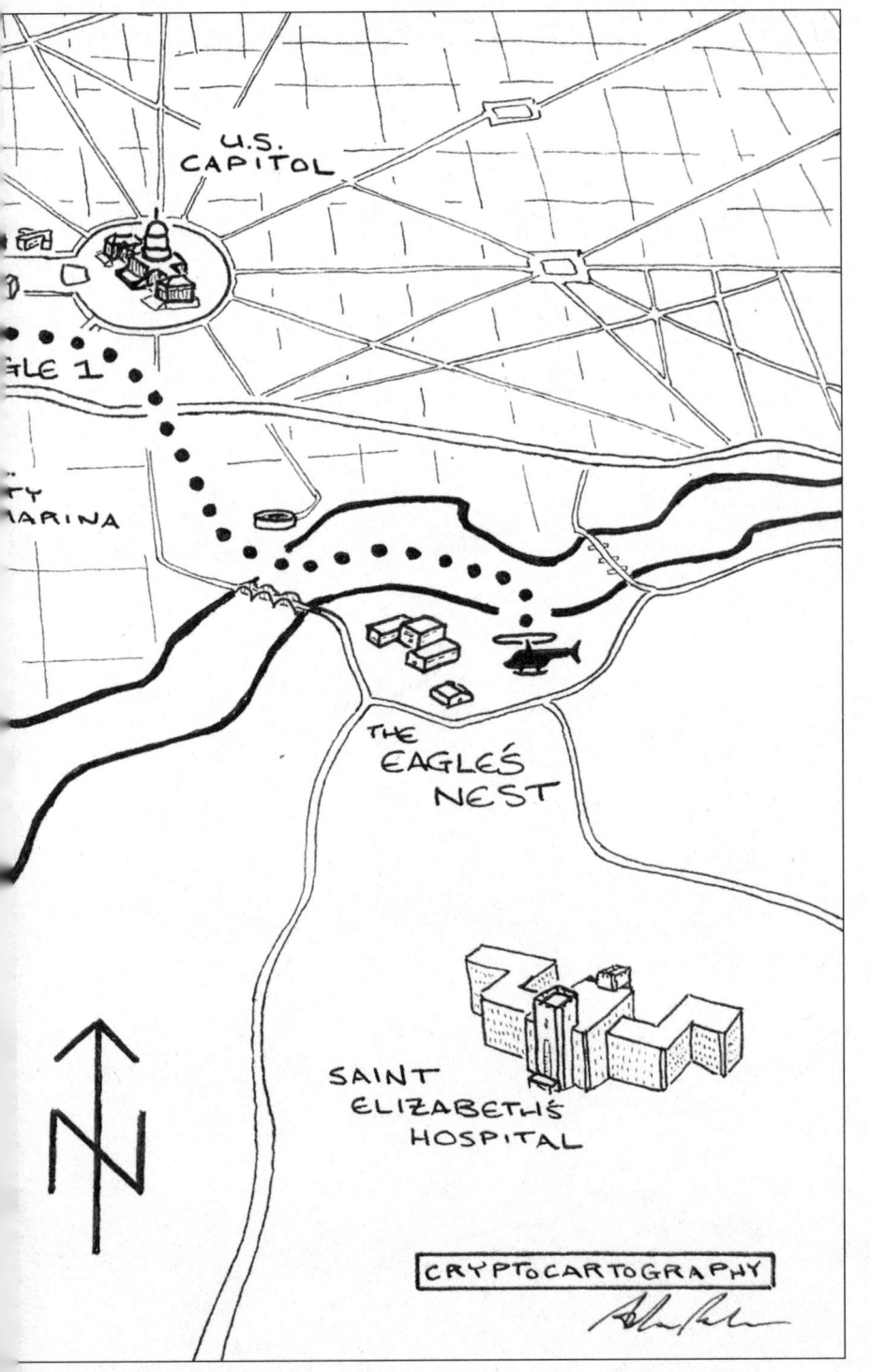

part one

———

January 13, 1982

Washington, DC, is a place unlike any other in the United States. It is a city of marble monuments and national treasures, the setting for spectacular neoclassical architecture and awe-inspiring panoramas.

Founded in 1790 as the national capital, the federal district was carved out of land ceded from two states: Maryland and Virginia. At one time a hundred square miles in area, it straddled the Potomac River at the confluence with the Eastern Branch, now known as the Anacostia River. Virginia's portion of the District of Columbia — thirty-two square miles including the city of Alexandria — was returned to the state in 1847.

Designed for the purpose of government, the District of Columbia is home to the White House, the Capitol, the Library of Congress, the Smithsonian Institution, and a panoply of federal agencies and departments from agriculture to the National Zoo. Washington is the stage for the dramas of politics, diplomacy, and power.

Washington is also a place of work, primarily the work of government. More than 340,000 federal workers are employed in the District of Columbia — cogs and gears in the vast alphabet engine that keeps the government functioning. Countless thousands of others work in Washington for trade groups, government contractors, think tanks, and a multitude of organizations and associations.

Washington is the epicenter of one of the highest-cost-of-living regions in the country, and few who work in the city actually live in it. People commute to Washington by road and by rail from the suburbs and beyond. The city's population swells and ebbs by the hundreds of thousands every weekday, a pulsating lifeblood of labor.

The personnel of the DC Fire Department's Engine Company 16 are unimpressed by the picturesque magnificence of the nation's capital. Iconic landmarks blend in as a routine part of the everyday cityscape. Firefighters have little time to reflect on their stately surroundings while racing to a fire or accident. To them, it's just a job. From the biggest city to the smallest town, a firefighter's work is essentially the same. In its simplest terms, put the wet stuff on the hot stuff.

Sergeant Joe Dean and the four other members of the Engine 16 crew were among more than a hundred firefighters and thirty pieces of equipment at the scene of a three-alarm fire at the former Upshur Street Clinic in northwest Washington on this Wednesday morning.

For more than thirty years, the Upshur Clinic had provided medical care to indigent Washington residents. After it closed in 1980, the five-story brick building fell prey to vagrancy. Now an arsonist had set a fire that quickly consumed the decrepit building in a blazing conflagration.

The first alarm was received just before 3:00 A.M. Fires at night are often the worst because people are asleep, giving the flames a long head start before being detected. Nearby buildings are often occupied by families who end up displaced by smoke or the drench of fire hoses.

The Upshur Clinic fire rapidly became so dire that the fire department activated its loathed Plan E — an emergency mobilization that keeps the present shift on duty and calls in the next shift early, temporarily doubling the number of personnel on duty. Plan E is only implemented in extreme cases to ensure that sufficient resources are in place to protect the rest of the city during a major incident. Firefighters poured water on the building in windchill dipping into single digits. One firefighter suffered frostbite and was taken to MedStar Washington Hospital Center for treatment.

By midmorning, when it was time to return to their station on 13th Street, Dean and his men grappled with frozen fire hoses too stiff to load back onto the engine. It was the second night in a row with a massive multiple-alarm fire in bitter-cold weather, a combination both exceedingly unpleasant and dangerous for firefighters. This was the coldest, most inhospitable weather Dean could recall in his thirteen years on the job.

What he and the crew of Engine Company 16 could not know was that they were only a third of the way through what would be the busiest twenty-four hours in the history of the DC Fire Department.

Huge swaths of the country were in the grips of a historic winter storm. A dip in the jet stream blasted arctic chill over the Midwest and East Coast. Chicago and Atlanta recorded their lowest temperatures of the twentieth century. The cold snap brought record cold to Florida, destroying $500 million in citrus crops. Three days earlier, on Sunday, January 10, the San Diego Chargers had played against the Cincinnati Bengals in Riverfront Stadium for the 1981 AFC Championship in the coldest game in NFL history — an air temperature of nine degrees below zero Fahrenheit with a windchill that made it feel like fifty-nine below. Washington's National Airport documented a temperature of two below, breaking a record low that had stood for forty years. It was a rare winter in which the Potomac River froze over with ice several inches thick.

During the second week of January, blizzards dumped snow on large stretches of the country, as far south as Alabama and Georgia. Several inches of snow remained on the ground in Washington, covering streets with sloppy slush.

Another major storm system was menacing the East Coast. A trough of low pressure was churning up from the Gulf of Mexico, an immense mass of warmer, humid air barreling northeast toward the Mid-Atlantic.

The National Weather Service, a unit of the Department of Commerce based just outside Washington in Silver Spring, Maryland, issued a forecast for a mixture of sleet and snow beginning in the morning and increasing in intensity during the afternoon, with a total new accumulation of six to eight inches expected by day's end.

Foul weather delayed morning commuters relying on the Washington Metropolitan Area Transit Authority (WMATA) Metrorail subway system, popularly known as Metro. Snow and ice prevented doors from closing, interfered with traction or "third rail" power pickup, and caused other mechanical problems, forcing twenty-seven trains out of service during the morning peak ridership period. Delays rippled throughout the system. It was shaping up to be the most chaotic day in Metro's six years of operation.

Metrorail was the latest of a new generation of urban rail systems developed after World War II, along with the Bay Area Rapid Transit (BART) system in San Francisco, which became operational in 1972, and the Metropolitan Atlanta Rapid Transit Authority (MARTA) subway system that opened in 1979. WMATA's Metro, like BART and MARTA, was a state-of-the-art computerized rail system designed for automatic control and operation, intended to run safely and efficiently with a minimum of human involvement.

Washingtonians embraced Metro when the subway began operating in 1976. Architect Harry Weese designed visually dramatic underground stations for the system, which featured coffered concrete barrel vault ceilings that created awe-inspiring cavernous spaces. Wide platforms allowed the flow of large numbers of people. Tickets were dispensed by vending machines to minimize lines. An attendant at each station was available for assistance if needed. Metro was the model of a modern urban rail system: clean and safe with a grandeur suited for the nation's capital.

From an initial 4.2-mile rail segment with five stations between Farragut North and Rhode Island Avenue, Metro expanded into a nearly 40-mile system with forty-three stations on three color-coded routes and an average of more than 290,000 riders per day.

The nerve center of Metro was the Operations Control Center (OCC), a windowless bunker-like room in WMATA's basement. The entire rail system could be monitored and controlled from the OCC. A bank of eight cathode-ray tube monitors displayed the status of every train and every point in the system. Facing the monitors was a three-sided wrap-around console with a constellation of buttons and switches that would look at home in the control room of a nuclear power station.

The center console had panels to run trains remotely, operate switches that moved trains from one track to another, and control power to the third rail for maintenance workers. To the right were panels for mobile radio communication with Metro supervisors and train conductors, as well as the public address system for each station. On the left console were panels for alarms and a printer to maintain a continuous log of events.

From this console, personnel known as controllers monitored trains throughout the system. If necessary, a train could be operated remotely from the OCC and safely advanced to the next station. When the system was working perfectly, humans weren't needed at all.

The Metrorail system was designed around computerization. Computers continually monitored fare and ticket collection, keeping track of how many riders were in the system at any moment.

Trains could be operated in full automatic mode with the assurance of efficiency and safety. This mode put computers in control of the speed of trains, the distance between trains, the time of arrival at a station, and how long a train remained at a station. When trains were running in full automatic mode, a conductor was only needed aboard to open and close doors and make announcements.

The OCC was designed for equipment, not for the comfort

of humans. When all was running smoothly, one controller could monitor the system and take over to run it manually if necessary. On this day, the OCC was cramped for space with the addition of supervisory controller Kenneth Banks, assistant superintendent Paul Hobgood Jr., and superintendent Joseph Earl Taylor, all scrambling to move trains and buses around to get the system back to normal status.

By late morning, Washington-area streets were slick with a mixture of sleet and freezing rain topped with a thickening layer of steadily falling snow.

Covering the weather was Chester Panzer's first assignment of the day. A videographer for WJLA-TV, Washington's ABC affiliate television station, Panzer was tasked with recording winter scenes for the noon news. He drove the station's crew car, an unmarked brown Oldsmobile sedan with a whip antenna mounted on the trunk, to pick up his soundman, George Patterson, at his home in the Washington suburbs.

Panzer and Patterson had worked together as a team for about a year in WJLA's public affairs and documentary unit. Due to staff shortages, they'd been temporarily reassigned to the news division. This was their second day in news, using somebody else's vehicle and equipment. Although all the cameras and recorders were the same makes and models, each device had its own quirks and idiosyncrasies. It takes time to get used to unfamiliar gear. But the assignment was an easy lift: simple bread-and-butter visuals to run in the background while the anchor delivered the news.

Both Panzer and Patterson had experience as videographers and as soundmen, so they took turns with the roles.

Today, Panzer was working the camera. Patterson's job was to carry the fifteen-pound video recording unit, slung from a strap across his shoulders, and hold a shotgun microphone to capture interviews and ambient audio.

The two spent time in the suburbs of Northern Virginia recording idyllic snowscapes, cars sliding through slush, and residents shoveling sidewalks and brushing off cars. Panzer then drove the crew car to the TV station at 1120 Connecticut Avenue, midway between Dupont Circle and the White House, and delivered the video on a three-quarter-inch cassette tape.

After a quick lunch, the assignment desk sent Panzer and Patterson to cover a house fire in Rockville. Upon arrival, they were surprised to find the house still fully engulfed in flames even though they had driven a considerable distance. Usually, fires are under control or extinguished by the time the press is on the scene. But frozen hydrants meant that firefighters were having difficulty getting water on the fire.

Panzer and Patterson had their own problems. After removing the equipment from the trunk, Panzer plugged a nine-foot cable into the back of the video camera and handed it to Patterson to plug the other end into the recording deck. The camera hoisted on his shoulder, Panzer put his eye to the viewfinder and hit the ROLL button at his fingertips. There was no flashing red light to indicate that the deck was recording. Frustrated, they switched the cable for another type that required the soundman to press the RECORD button on the deck. Still nothing. Patterson looked down and saw that the connector had fallen off the cable, which was detached and spooled on the ground. They found a third cable that finally worked and recorded firefighters dousing the house, which was still in flames.

On the way to bring the tape to WJLA, Panzer wondered what other challenges might be lurking ahead for them. He could not have imagined that by day's end he would record a riveting life-and-death drama broadcast around the world.

1:00 P.M.

Cleared of the Upshur Clinic fire scene, Engine 16 returned to its station at 1018 13th Street NW. Dean supervised the crew as they wiped down the equipment and replaced tanks of compressed air on the Scott breathing apparatus. Hoses were laid out on the firehouse equipment room floor to thaw so they could be reloaded onto the vehicles, while everyone looked forward to the warm lunch that was being prepared upstairs.

Engine Co. 16 was the largest firehouse in Washington. Known as the Big House, the three-story brick Colonial Revival station stood out against the neighboring classical architecture. It was the only station with four equipment bays — room for Engine 16, aerial truck Tower 3, Ambulance 16, a battalion chief, and the deputy chief of operations.

The second floor of the station housed the living quarters, along with a kitchen and a rec room with a television set. The third floor, where the fire department operated its own medical clinic, could be accessed through a separate entrance in the back. The facility included doctors' offices, an operating room and recovery room, and a dental clinic. Police officers and firefighters could get work-related injuries treated at the clinic, as well as physical exams tied to their jobs.

Caught up with his tasks, firefighter John Leck leaned against the heavy wooden doors of the Engine 16 bay and looked out the window. Snow was falling so heavily, he could barely see across 13th Street. He watched cars slowly wending through a swirling mass of flakes.

"It's snowing like a mother out there," Leck muttered to himself. Not a good day to be going anywhere.

It was just as well. Because of Plan E, he wasn't going home anytime soon.

Joe Stiley had been following weather reports closely all morning. It was one of the worst snowstorms he'd ever seen in the Washington area. He was supposed to fly out of Washington National Airport that afternoon, but the blizzard was casting his plans in doubt.

Stiley, forty-three years old, was a vice president of General Telephone and Electronics (GTE), where he managed the development of computerized telecommunications systems for corporate clients and the government — including classified projects. The work suited Stiley's structured way of thinking.

A former US Navy pilot, Stiley had studied computer science as an undergraduate at University of California–

Los Angeles on the GI Bill. He completed his master's in engineering management at UC San Diego in 1964 and went to work in the private sector.

For the navy, Stiley flew a Douglas A-1 Skyraider, a single-seat low-wing propeller-powered attack plane that was a mainstay of carrier-based aircraft. After his military service, he worked as a flight instructor and often flew as a private pilot.

He was traveling with his administrative assistant, Patricia "Nikki" Felch. They had tickets for Air Florida Flight 90 to Tampa, scheduled to depart National at 2:15 P.M. They arrived at the airport early enough to eat lunch before takeoff.

Stiley's twenty-eight-year-old assistant was in a good mood. Felch and her fiancé had set a date for their marriage — May 15 — and she was looking forward to a break from the miserable winter weather, packing a bathing suit to take advantage of the hotel's pool and bask in the warm Florida sunshine.

Stiley was not looking forward to the trip. Today was the twelfth birthday of his son, Jay. He wished he could be there to celebrate with his family. But work always came first to a driven, objective-oriented person like him. He didn't expect to be lounging in the sun. In his briefcase, Stiley brought his checkbook and bills to pay, as well as other work requiring his attention.

The purpose of their trip was grim but unavoidable. GTE was closing a facility in St. Petersburg. The company could retain a few engineers and relocate them to other divisions, but a lot of people were going to be put out of work. It was Stiley's job to deliver the bad news.

"Smoking or nonsmoking?" the ticket agent asked at the Air Florida counter as they checked in. Stiley smoked Pall Malls. Felch was a nonsmoker. They brokered an agreement to fly in the smoking section on the way down and nonsmoking on the return trip.

More than three dozen law enforcement agencies are authorized within the sixty-eight square miles of the District of Columbia. The Metropolitan Police Department has jurisdiction over most city streets and non-governmental buildings. The Secret Service is responsible for the area around the White House, and the US Capitol Police are tasked with securing the other end of Pennsylvania Avenue. The Federal Bureau of Investigation, the Bureau of Alcohol, Tobacco, and Firearms, and military police at various bases and facilities around the city are among the others.

The oldest uniformed federal law enforcement agency in the country is the US Park Police, established by George Washington in 1791 to protect federal properties. Park police have jurisdiction over large portions of the District of Columbia, including the National Mall and public areas such as Rock Creek Park and the C&O Canal, the Baltimore-Washington and George Washington Parkways, federal facilities such as the Beltsville Agricultural Research Center in Maryland, and federal parks throughout the country. As sworn officers, park police also have law enforcement authority in Virginia and Maryland.

The chief pilot of the park police aviation unit, Don

Usher, was classified as emergency essential personnel and did not have the luxury of staying home from work during the storm. He allowed extra time for the twenty-nine-mile drive from his home in Gambrills, Maryland, to work in the southeast corner of Washington.

Usher, thirty-one, had been flying helicopters most of his adult life. He joined the army after qualifying for warrant officer rotary-wing flight school while a senior at Catonsville High School in a suburb of Baltimore. With a war raging halfway across the world in Vietnam, Usher figured he'd be better off flying over the battlefield than walking through it.

The crucible of Vietnam honed Usher's piloting skills. He flew Bell UH-1 "Huey" helicopters for combat assault missions and troop support, learning to navigate in tight jungle clearings and while under fire.

For three months, Usher flew a Hughes OH-6A Cayuse, a light and agile scout helicopter, on extremely risky hunter-killer missions. The Cayuse pilots were used as bait, buzzing suspected enemy positions to draw small-arms fire and reveal their locations for Bell AH-1 Cobra attack helicopters to swoop in and eliminate them. Of 1,419 Cayuse built for the Vietnam War, 842 were shot down or crashed during low-level flights. Usher was shot down by ground fire in the Boi Loi Woods northwest of Cu Chi while on a hunter-killer mission. Two bullets struck, but did not penetrate, his body armor. His helicopter was destroyed. Usher was awarded the Distinguished Flying Cross for his actions.

Following his discharge from the military, Usher returned to Baltimore. His older brother Mike, a Maryland State

Police officer, suggested that he apply to fly helicopters in the department's aviation division. But he fell short of the minimum height requirement for the Maryland State Police by an eighth of an inch. Then he learned that the US Park Police were going to begin flying helicopters and didn't care if its officers were slightly less than five foot nine.

Typical for rookie park police officers, Usher's first detail was in central DC, in and around the National Mall. Working with millions of tourists who visit the capital, providing directions and explaining the various landmarks, invariably makes park police officers interpretive historians as much as they are cops.

Usher was detailed to traffic enforcement on the George Washington Memorial Parkway and the Baltimore-Washington Parkway until he was accepted into the park police aviation unit. Established in 1973, the aviation unit maintains two helicopters at a facility shared with the Maryland State Police aviation division in Anacostia Park in southeast Washington. The base is known as the Eagle's Nest. Usher was the pilot of Eagle One, a Bell 206L LongRanger II helicopter with the registration number N22PP.

The aviation unit's primary mission was to serve as law enforcement in the complicated Washington, DC, airspace. Eighty percent of the unit's missions are routine police operations providing support for law enforcement on the ground. The blue-and-white helicopters are seen overhead whenever the presidential motorcade rolls through town. Park police helicopters also perform medevac flights for the sick and injured, landing in places like Great Falls or Rock

Creek Park and airlifting to MedStar Washington Hospital Center or Shock Trauma in Baltimore.

Usher kept a steady hand on his steering wheel while driving down the Baltimore-Washington Parkway. All he had to do was get to the Eagle's Nest safely in time for his 3:00 P.M. shift.

1:30 P.M.

At 1900 E Street, NW, three blocks west of the White House, stood a nondescript seven-story building so utilitarian that it was designated only as Federal Office Building 9. The US Office of Personnel Management (OPM), the human resources agency for the federal government, was located inside. The OPM's responsibilities include making decisions about federal employees during local emergencies such as storms and natural disasters, balancing the need for the continuity of essential government services against the safety of employees and the public.

Key personnel — the OPM's resource management officer, director for emergency management, and director for personnel security, among others — huddled all morning in the agency's emergency operations office. They pored over information from the National Weather Service and field reports from the highway departments in the District, Maryland, and Virginia; state police in Maryland and Virginia; and local police agencies in the city and surrounding suburbs.

Roads across the region had become slick in just a few hours. Traffic accidents were so numerous that police departments were only responding to the most serious crashes — those with injured victims. Conditions were so bad that Virginia closed government offices in Richmond, a hundred miles to the south, at noon. With the bulk of the storm still approaching, snowfall was expected to become much heavier around midafternoon with a total snow accumulation of up to eight inches. It became clear that the longer federal employees remained at work, the more dangerous their trips home would become.

The OPM decided at 1:30 to dismiss all nonessential federal employees three hours early in the interest of safety. The decision triggered a telephone tree of notifications to spread the word to federal offices in the Washington area.

Because the early dismissal meant that rush hour would occur three hours sooner than usual, the OPM as a matter of routine also notified the WMATA, the DC police department, the Office of Emergency Preparedness, and other agencies affected by the decision.

Since joining the District of Columbia government as director of transportation, Thomas Downs had found some aspects of his job more fulfilling than others. Previously the executive director of the US Urban Mass Transportation Administration under President Carter, Downs particularly enjoyed working on the renovation of Daniel Burnham's landmark Union Station and the expansion of the Metrorail system. He had less appetite for the public furor that arose whenever changes were made to street parking rules in residential neighborhoods, which precipitated death threats and at least one attempt at burning down his home.

On this day, Downs's primary focus was trying to keep traffic moving on the streets of Washington. All day, like a wartime general, he had been deploying his fleet of trucks to plow and spread sand on major avenues. Trying to keep up with the heavy accumulation blanketing the city was a losing battle.

When he received notification from the OPM about the early release of employees, Downs initiated protocols to facilitate the flow of traffic out of the city. He reversed lanes on the major bridges to Virginia and switched the traffic signal system into the evening rush-hour pattern. The changes take awhile to propagate throughout the system and would not be in place until about 3:00 P.M., which would be cutting it close.

Had anybody asked, Downs would have recommended against early release at such a late hour. It takes time to prepare for the evening rush hour, especially on a day like this. The lights and signals wouldn't be ready. The streets wouldn't be cleared of snow, and some side streets would remain impassable.

WMATA general manager Richard Page told the OPM that his agency was unable to move up the afternoon peak service period, which was regularly 3:30 to 6:30 P.M. By agreement with the District of Columbia, the WMATA must be notified by 8:00 A.M. on a day of early release.

The WMATA had about 1,510 buses and 256 railcars in service during peak periods, with three to five minutes between trains. During off-peak hours, they had half as many trains and one-third as many buses running, with six to ten minutes between trains.

Ramping up wasn't as easy as flipping a switch. It took four to six hours for the WMATA to mobilize for full peak-period service, Page told the OPM. The OCC was still dealing with equipment problems and late trains. Buses were stranded throughout the city. Gearing up for peak service would mean having equipment readied and put in place and calling in two thousand additional employees early — during a blizzard. Little could be done to make things happen sooner. Trains and buses would remain at their off-peak schedule until 3:30, and they would consequently be more crowded than normal.

1:38 P.M.

Snow fell heavily in the afternoon, accumulating at a rate of one to two inches per hour. Washington National Airport temporarily closed to allow snowplows to clear the airfield. Dozens of flights were delayed or diverted to other airports.

Anticipating a brief airport closure, Air Florida began boarding for the 2:15 flight to Tampa at Gate 12.

Air Florida 90's seventy-four passengers represented a cross section of ages, socioeconomic classes, and backgrounds. They included businesspeople, retirees, one of the country's foremost butterfly experts, and eight active military service members — one of whom had a briefcase handcuffed to his wrist.

Among the first to board were twenty-four-year-old Jose Tirado, his twenty-two-year-old wife, Priscilla, and their nine-week-old baby, Jason. The Tirados met in Spain in 1976, when Priscilla's father, Beirne Keefer, was based overseas with the US Navy. They married four years later. In June 1981, Priscilla returned to America to have her baby, staying with her grandmother in College Park, Maryland.

Jose joined the family in College Park in October and within a week landed a job with a contractor working on the driveway of Vice President George H. W. Bush's residence at the US Naval Observatory. Priscilla's father, retired from the navy and now running an import business in Clearwater, Florida, was sponsoring Jose for immigration. Jose had an appointment at the immigration office in Tampa on January 15.

The Tirados were excited about starting their new life in Clearwater. The flight — only the second time Jose had been on a plane, other than his trip from Madrid — was the final step in an adventure that had taken years.

Priscilla had reduced her smoking during the pregnancy but still wanted to be able to smoke during the flight. Since she enjoyed watching the wing's control surfaces move during takeoff and landing, Jose, an adoring husband and doting father, indulged his wife's wishes and let her have the window seat in the first row of the smoking section, 17F, while he sat next to her in 17E with Jason on his lap.

Arland Williams, a forty-seven-year-old bank examiner for the Federal Reserve in Atlanta, was headed home after meeting with the Federal Reserve Board of Governors about a troubled Florida bank. For the past year, he had been working with Metropolitan Bank and Trust of Tampa, which was teetering on failure.

Looking out the jet bridge window as he boarded Flight 90, Joe Stiley, the GTE vice president and former navy pilot, noticed tire tracks in the snow around the plane, but no footprints. The crew didn't perform a preflight visual inspection of the aircraft — one of the first things taught in flight school. Stiley couldn't help but judge. *Get out there and do your job*, he thought.

Walking back to the smoking section, Stiley's assistant, Nikki Felch, took a window seat, 18A, and Stiley took the aisle seat next to her, 18C.

Last to board was forty-one-year-old Bert Hamilton, a purchasing supervisor for Fairchild Industries. One of eight employees of Fairchild's space and electronics division en route to a Honeywell facility in Tampa, Hamilton walked down the aisle past his colleagues to sit in the last row of the plane, in the aisle seat to the right, 21D. Although not a smoker, Hamilton held the belief that the rear of an airplane is the safest in the event of a crash.

Once all passengers were aboard, there was nothing to do but wait for the airport to reopen and resume operations. During the long wait, Stiley tried to get interested in a book he had brought along. It was difficult to focus on the words on the page, with four babies aboard an increasingly warm and stuffy airliner.

After a while, a truck pulled alongside and briefly rinsed snow off one side of the plane with pinkish fluid, then stopped. Felch watched slush run down the window to her left. Later, the truck returned and hosed down the fuselage and both wings.

St. Elizabeths Hospital is a psychiatric institution operated by the National Institute of Mental Health located in the southeast corner of the District of Columbia on a bluff overlooking the confluence of the Anacostia and Potomac Rivers. More than a hundred buildings were scattered over the 346-acre campus, some dating to its founding as the Government Hospital for the Insane in 1852.

Maintaining St. Elizabeths' aging buildings in good condition required a cadre of skilled workers: carpenters, electricians, plumbers, and others useful with tools. Roger Olian was foreman of the institution's seven-person sheet metal and roofing department.

Naturally athletic and six foot three, the thirty-four-year-old Olian looked every bit of the ex-marine that he was. Thoughtful and soft-spoken, he had never been one to back down from a challenge. When he graduated college in 1969, at the height of the Vietnam War, he lost his student deferment. A week later, he was drafted. Given the opportunity to select in which branch of the military he wanted to serve, Olian chose the marines.

"I had to serve because I was afraid," he said. "I didn't know how I'd react in war. I had to know if I could handle it."

Olian spent two years in Vietnam wielding an M79

grenade launcher, a devastating weapon that made him a target for enemy fire. While on patrol with his squad during the rainy season, he traversed a raging, flooded river and tumbled over a waterfall to save the life of a medic who was near drowning. Confident in his abilities as a strong swimmer, Olian took the risk.

Days later, Olian's squad encountered dozens of Vietnamese civilians taking refuge on a barren hill that was the only dry ground on the flooded landscape. They had no shelter or food and huddled together in a relentless downpour. The squad had a large tent that a couple of marines decided to set up. As the tent was being raised, a teenage girl walked up to Olian with two small children who were naked, starving, and cold. The girl didn't understand English, and Olian knew very little Vietnamese. Language wasn't necessary. She handed the children to Olian, who held them shivering against his chest under his poncho until the tent was ready, unable to do more than share body heat and respite from the rain.

"If this is the only reason why I'm over here, the trip was worth it," he told himself.

Born on February 9, Olian's astrological sign was Aquarius, the water-bearer. Water had been a recurring element during significant moments of his life. This would be one of those days.

When word filtered through St. Elizabeths that federal employees were being released early, Olian's first thought was to call his wife, Donna, who worked at a navy recruiting station in Crystal City, Virginia.

"If they don't let you out pretty soon, just leave and go home because the weather is getting really bad," he told her. "If you don't leave soon, you're going to be spending hours and hours on the road."

On the other side of the Potomac, in Arlington, Aldo De La Cruz was riding along with his buddy Steve Raynes in Mike Patterson's car. The three airmen worked together at the Pentagon. Released from work three hours early along with other federal employees, the men were going to Bolling Air Force Base to play racquetball, seven miles away in southeast Washington.

De La Cruz had ended up in the capital because of a misunderstanding. Enlisting in the US Air Force with a couple of years of college computer classes under his belt, De La Cruz was given the opportunity to choose his assignment. He picked a detail in Washington because he thought it would be close to his family in Portland, Oregon. But he had selected an assignment that based him in the Washington on the other side of the country, the District of Columbia. His first time away from home, at the age of nineteen, De La Cruz found himself performing mainframe computing services for the Joint Chiefs of Staff in a classified facility in the Pentagon.

The largest employer in Northern Virginia, the Pentagon employs more than twenty-four thousand people. It is so huge that six shopping-mall-sized parking lots are needed to hold the thousands of vehicles of its workers. As employees were released from the Pentagon that day, a seemingly endless stream of cars flowed onto city streets and nearby expressways.

The three airmen couldn't do anything but inch along with traffic toward I-395 into Washington, and listen to music.

2:53 P.M.

With the runways and taxiways plowed, National Airport reopened for flights. The crew of Flight 90 told passengers they were in line waiting for departure.

Joe Stiley had struck up a conversation with two students sitting across the aisle returning to school after winter break. The air in the plane was warm and stifling. He removed his jacket and set it on the empty seat between him and Nikki Felch, closing his eyes and resting while they waited.

Bert Hamilton spent some time observing a young couple sitting in front of him. They couldn't keep their hands off each other, hugging and kissing. *They can't be married*, he thought. *It's a new relationship.*

Priscilla Tirado anxiously kept glancing at the NO SMOK-ING sign overhead.

At 3:00 P.M., city transportation director Thomas Downs bundled up and went outside to check the status of traffic flow changes for the afternoon rush hour. He found that most lane indicators on bridges to Virginia were properly set outbound from the city, except for on the Cabin John Bridge and the 14th Street Bridge.

Downs walked several blocks around his office and along the National Mall. Snowfall was at its heaviest, accumulating at a rate of two or more inches an hour throughout the region, blizzard-like conditions. Traffic in the downtown area was at an absolute standstill. There was hardly any movement on the major arteries like Constitution, Independence, and Pennsylvania Avenues, and 12th and 9th Streets. Many side streets were impassable, with cars hopelessly stranded. The afternoon rush hour was going to be an awful mess.

A rescue technician for the park police aviation unit, forty-one-year-old Melvin "Gene" Windsor, drove cautiously from his home near Frederick, Maryland, for his 3:00 P.M. shift at the Eagle's Nest. On a good day, the drive would take about an hour. Windsor allotted an extra hour today for the treacherous road conditions.

A Washington-area native who grew up in Rockville, Maryland, Windsor joined the park police in 1971 after an unfulfilling career as a carpet store manager. His park police career began with patrol duties in Washington, then traffic enforcement on the George Washington Memorial and the Baltimore-Washington Parkways. Seeking a more interesting assignment, Windsor began training for the motorcycle division until knee pain forced him to quit.

Windsor saw an opening in the park police aviation unit, which seemed like an interesting duty. He was selected for the position even though he had no medical or aviation experience and was almost a decade older than his peers in the unit. Windsor undertook paramedic training through the DC Fire Department at MedStar Washington Hospital Center and joined the aviation unit in 1979.

He hadn't made it far down I-270 toward DC when a driver entering the expressway from a ramp lost control, skidded across three lanes, and bounced his car off the Jersey barrier directly into Windsor's path. Unable to stop in time, Windsor plowed into the wayward vehicle.

Nobody was injured in the collision, but a passenger in the other car was rattled. Windsor's car sustained minor front-end damage. Had the angle of impact been slightly different, the car could have been disabled and prevented him from going to work. After an exchange of information and twenty-five wasted minutes, Windsor continued on his way.

Despite his best efforts, Windsor would arrive late for his shift at the Eagle's Nest. Traffic was so bad that it took an hour to drive the last five miles from the Tidal Basin to Anacostia Park. Windsor was assigned to Eagle Two, a Bell LongRanger II. The pilot of Eagle Two, Robert Hartley, was still stuck on the road and hadn't made it to work yet. Pilot Don Usher and paramedic Ron Galey went over the preflight checks for Eagle One.

As the aviation unit's chief pilot, Usher had the final word on whether the park police would be flying, and he had already decided against taking the helicopters out under present conditions. The latest report from the National Weather Service indicated a ceiling — the bottom of the cloud level — of only two hundred feet and visibility of a quarter mile.

Lacking many of the instruments that allow planes to

fly in poor weather, the park service helicopters flew under visual flight rules. The current conditions were outside mini- mum acceptable guidelines for safe helicopter flight. Every- body was grounded — the park service, Maryland State Police, Metro Police, even Marine One. Nobody was flying.

Still, Usher and the others made sure Eagle One and Eagle Two were fully fueled, properly equipped, and ready to go. The weather would break sooner or later. Until then, their job was to be prepared.

With the weather looming as the major event of the day, the WJLA newsroom assignment desk dispatched Panzer and Patterson to National Airport to interview travelers inconve- nienced by the airport's closure. The pair drove to the airport and met up with Josh Mankiewicz, the on-air reporter, who took the Metro from the station on Connecticut Avenue. With Panzer behind the camera and Patterson working the mic, Mankiewicz spoke with several travelers about delayed or canceled flights and the effect on their plans.

By 3:30, their work was completed. Mankiewicz took the videotape and returned to WJLA by Metro. With no more pending assignments, the videographer and soundman were done for the day. Panzer and Patterson got back in the crew car and headed north on the George Washington Memorial Parkway, which had been reduced to a single lane moving at a fitful crawl. Panzer was going to drop off Patterson at home in Alexandria, then drive to his own home in Burke, Virginia. Traffic was an endless ribbon of red brake lights as far as the eye could see. Patterson set the heat to high, tuned the radio to a music station, and settled in for a long ride home.

Passengers aboard Air Florida Flight 90 grew restless as the airport ground crew had difficulty pulling the plane away from the gate. The tug that was supposed to push them back did not have chains on its tires and could not get traction. Over the public address system, a flight attendant told passengers that they would be on their way as soon as another tug pushed the plane back.

After several minutes, passengers felt the plane move backward and turn, then slowly roll toward the taxiway. Several jets were ahead of them in line for departure.

Roger Olian was in a foul mood. He'd been driving his beat-up Datsun pickup for nearly two hours through tortuous bumper-to-bumper traffic. The drive had been a slog all the way from St. Elizabeths Hospital up the Baltimore-Washington Parkway along the Anacostia River to the Southeast Expressway, which turns into I-395 heading toward Virginia.

With his gas gauge hovering near empty, Olian was determined to keep his truck running. He urgently needed to get off the interstate and find a gas station. His battery was going bad, too, so if he ran out of gas there might not be enough juice to start the engine again. To help conserve fuel, Olian turned off the radio and turned the windshield wipers off as long as he was just sitting in traffic. Snow blanketed the hood of his truck.

Traffic was so painfully slow that as 4:00 P.M. approached, Olian was just about where he would have been had he left work at the usual time — crossing the 14th Street Bridge over the Potomac River. It seemed like he'd been sitting there forever. If the traffic would just keep moving across the bridge, Olian could get off the interstate for gas.

3:59 P.M.

When the Flight 90 passengers who had been cooped up for almost two hours heard, "Ladies and gentlemen, we have just been cleared on the runway for takeoff. Flight attendants, please be seated," their relief was palpable. The airliner rolled down Runway 36, slowly gaining speed. Lumbering through the slush that had built up on the tarmac felt like driving down a rutted country road.

Joe Stiley sensed something was wrong almost immediately. He had flown on 737s many times and knew what a normal takeoff felt like. He wasn't being pushed into his seat as forcefully as he expected. The engines didn't seem to be going as fast as they ought to be.

Bert Hamilton, seated in the last row, looked over his shoulder at the flight attendant in the crew seat. She shrugged at him, showing no outward sign of concern. He reached down and tightened the seat belt on his lap.

The ground roll lasted way too long. It didn't feel like the plane was accelerating enough to lift off the runway, moving so slowly that Stiley expected the captain to cut the throttle and reject the takeoff.

When he saw National's VHF omnidirectional range

(VOR) beacon facility, near the end of Runway 36, go past the window, Stiley was sure that a crash was imminent. They were running out of runway.

"We're in trouble. Go like this," he told Nikki Felch, tucking his face between his knees and covering his head with his arms.

Air Florida 90's nose slowly rose from the tarmac, the engines droning as the plane sluggishly took to the air.

Almost immediately after leaving the ground, the plane began to shudder. Many passengers assumed the shaking was due to turbulence that would soon pass. Priscilla Tirado, more experienced with air travel than her husband, clasped his hand and reassured him that the disturbance was normal.

Stiley was astonished that the plane was airborne. There was no discernible upward pitch to the aircraft. He raised his head to peek out the window.

We're at treetop level, he saw with alarm.

The galley and overhead bins clattered louder as the shuddering grew more violent. It felt as though the plane was shaking itself apart.

Stiley realized that the plane was in a stall and about to crash. He knew that National Airport's departing flight path followed the course of the Potomac River to avoid restricted airspace around the White House and Capitol.

There are bridges ahead, Stiley thought. *God help us.*

Joe Carluccio, a Fairchild colleague sitting several rows ahead, turned to look back at Bert Hamilton with a weak smile on his face, shaking his head. Looking out the window to his left, Hamilton saw the stream of car taillights on

George Washington Parkway, and a bridge. The ground loomed closer, rising up to meet the plane. He felt the plane pitch upward and gripped the armrest of his seat.

Passengers screamed as the plane fell from the sky. Nikki Felch was lifted in her seat and saw eighteen rows of seats in front of her, all the way to the front of the plane.

Those aboard Flight 90 felt a relatively modest thump, as though being rear-ended in a car, then a jolting impact like a hard punch to the body.

A fleeting thought flashed through Stiley's mind — regret that his son's birthday would forever be the anniversary of his death — and awareness that he was tumbling through space still strapped in his seat.

Before the next thought could form, a powerful smash knocked Stiley unconscious.

part two

Palm 90

Captain Larry M. Wheaton rolled the Air Florida airliner, a Boeing 737 with the registration number N62AF, to a stop on the apron at Gate 12. He spooled down the engines and turned off a red warning light to let ground crew know that the plane was safe to approach. Flight 95 had arrived at Washington National Airport.

After refueling and boarding new passengers, the airliner would head to Fort Lauderdale, with an intermediate stop in Tampa, as Flight 90 — known by its air traffic control designation as Palm 90 — with a scheduled departure time of 2:15 P.M.

Flight 90 was a regular daily route flown by Air Florida. Among travel agents, Flight 90 was considered a "hot route" — a bargain for Washington-area travelers going to Florida. Flights were often booked full.

Miami-based Air Florida began operations as a cut-rate airline in 1972 with a single Boeing 707 jetliner. The carrier was launched with $12 fares from Miami to Orlando or St. Petersburg, to which the traveling public responded with enthusiasm. As an intrastate airline, Air Florida was not subject to the Civilian Aeronautics Board, the federal agency that regulated commercial aviation services such as routes and fares.

Air Florida lost money during its first seven years of operation. The airline kept costs down by purchasing used aircraft, outsourcing airport ground services, and eliminating frills such as in-flight food or drink services.

In 1978, the Airline Deregulation Act transformed the commercial airline industry. The law abolished federal regulation of fares and routes and lowered barriers to market entry for new airlines. Deregulation was intended to benefit the public by increasing competition, lowering airfares, and giving passengers more choices.

Air Florida moved swiftly under the new law, undercutting larger airlines with $50 fares between Miami and Philadelphia or Washington, DC. These new routes contributed to its first modest profit of $2.4 million in 1979. The next year, Air Florida had a fleet of ten Boeing 737s and five McDonnell Douglas DC-9s. It introduced flights to the Caribbean, Europe, and Central America.

In 1981, the airline expanded to Boston, Chicago, Newark, New York, and Toledo. The carrier remained in the black despite an economic recession and fierce competition for passengers. About a hundred employees were laid off during the last quarter of the year, mostly at its Miami headquarters.

By January 1982, Air Florida expected its third consecutive profitable year. The carrier boasted a fleet of twenty-five 737s, five 727s, four DC-10s, and three DC-9s. Going forward, the airline planned ambitious growth with more routes.

1:38 P.M.

Nine minutes after the Air Florida plane landed, National Airport closed to clear the airfield of snow. The snow was falling heavily, at a rate of about an inch an hour. Trucks plowed the runways, and taxiways and spread sand.

The delay allowed the crew aboard Flight 90 to relax while preparing for the next load of passengers. Wheaton talked with airport ground personnel while the plane was refueled with 1,567 gallons of jet fuel.

Neither Wheaton nor First Officer Roger A. Pettit had extensive experience flying a Boeing 737, and even less in winter weather.

Wheaton, thirty-four, had about eighty-three hundred flight hours as a pilot, mostly with piston-engine planes such as the Douglas DC-3. Flying since the age of eighteen, Wheaton enlisted in the army and piloted small single- and twin-engine propeller planes. He began flying the jet-powered DC-9 as first officer when he joined Air Florida in 1978 and had accumulated about 1,850 hours flying a Boeing 737.

Wheaton's advancement with Air Florida was rapid by industry standards. Most airlines promoted a copilot to captain after several years of experience. Wheaton was promoted to captain after working as copilot for fourteen months, with only 1,223 hours of experience in the cockpit of a jet.

Peers described Wheaton as an average pilot, with good operational skills. But his record was not without blemish. During a May 1980 flight test, he was found lacking in several areas including adherence to regulations, checklist usage, and flight procedures. He was suspended as captain until passing the test in August 1980, then reinstated. Wheaton received an unsatisfactory grade in an April 1981 proficiency test for deficiencies in knowledge of aircraft systems and limitations. He repeated the proficiency test three days later and passed.

Roger A. Pettit, the thirty-one-year-old first officer, had even less experience flying the 737. Prior to joining Air Florida in 1980, Pettit was an F-15 fighter pilot and flight instructor in the air force. He had about 3,350 flight hours of experience as a pilot, 990 hours of which were flying a 737.

Neither pilot had much experience flying a 737 in winter weather. Wheaton had taken off or landed in snowy, freezing conditions eight times in his career; Pettit, only twice.

A winter snowstorm was also a novelty for the flight attendants. Donna Adams, the twenty-three-year-old senior flight attendant, grew up in an aviation family. Her father was an ex-navy pilot who worked as an air traffic controller at a Miami-area executive airport, and her uncle led the San Jose Airman's Association in California. Adams was going on her fourth year with Air Florida.

Whenever possible, Adams scheduled flights with junior attendant Marilyn Nichols, twenty-five, her best friend. Nichols had worked for Air Florida since 1979. Recently learning that she was two months' pregnant with her first child, Nichols faced the necessity of having to notify the airlines and leave the work she enjoyed so much. This would be one of her last flights.

Like Adams, twenty-two-year-old junior flight attendant Kelly Duncan was raised in an aviation family. Her father, Jerry Duncan, was a pilot for Delta Air Lines, and her stepmother, Joan, worked for Air Florida. She began flight attendant training right after high school and had previously flown for Air Sunshine, a regional carrier acquired by Air Florida.

Living in Miami with two roommates and a cat, Duncan enjoyed the lifestyle of a free-spirited independent young woman. The previous weekend, she had gone bar-hopping with friends from Miami to the Keys.

Duncan remained aboard the 737 while Adams and Nichols stepped outside to frolic in the snow. It was their first experience with a blizzard.

Managed and operated by the Federal Aviation Administration (FAA), Washington National Airport had the reputation among pilots and aviation experts as one of the most dangerous in the United States.

"I have been an air force pilot. I have flown airplanes all my life," Virginia congressman Stanford Parris said during a September 1981 House hearing on safety at National Airport. "That is the lousiest airport in the world."

Located on a lobe of reclaimed land extending from the mudflats at a bend of the Potomac River, National Airport is surrounded on three sides by water.

The airport was so small that only one runway, the north-south-oriented Runway 36, was long enough for medium-haul commercial airliners. Ninety percent of air carriers used Runway 36. At 6,869 feet in length, it was the shortest main runway at any major airport in the United States. Two other shorter runways were used by private planes and other general aviation.

National Airport was also one of the busiest in the country. Fourteen million travelers passed through the small, outdated terminal every year — seven times the volume of the newer and more spacious Dulles International Airport twenty-six miles distant in rural Virginia.

With more than eight hundred daily takeoffs and landings, Runway 36 was the busiest runway in America. A plane took off or landed on it every sixty seconds during most of the day. By necessity, planes were managed by air traffic controllers with clockwork precision. A snag at any point could cause delays throughout the system.

National's tight confines allowed little room for error. Airport runways have paved areas at each end, called overruns, that provide a margin of safety in the event a pilot is forced to reject a takeoff or is unable to stop the plane before reaching the end. The FAA recommended that airport runways have an overrun of at least a thousand feet. The northern end of Runway 36 had a two-hundred-foot overrun, then a ten-foot drop to the Potomac. The overrun at the southern end was 375 feet.

Ideally, the trajectory of an airliner at takeoff is straight ahead at full speed. Pilots departing from National Airport cannot do that. The airspace over Washington is among the most highly restricted in the country. A prohibited zone, known as a P-56 restricted airspace, extends over the National Mall from the Lincoln Memorial to the US Capitol, and includes the White House, 2.5 miles north from the end of Runway 36.

To minimize the noise in neighboring residential communities, planes departing from National Airport are required to take a tortuous zigzagging route following the Potomac River upstream, making five turns at precise points over the water.

The first turn is a forty-degree bank to the left about a half mile out from the airport, approaching a series of six bridges crossing the Potomac between Washington and Northern Virginia. The first is called Long Bridge, a two-track rail bridge for freight and passenger trains. Running parallel to Long Bridge is a rail bridge for Metro's Yellow Line.

Next is a complex of spans known as the 14th Street Bridge, a major artery carrying I-395 over the Potomac. The 14th Street Bridge is actually three bridges — one each for northbound and southbound traffic, and the middle span for high-occupancy vehicles (HOV), with the direction changing for morning and afternoon rush-hour traffic. More than 180,000 vehicles traversed the 14th Street Bridge every day.

Farther upstream are the Arlington Memorial Bridge by the Lincoln Memorial, famous from state funeral processions to Arlington National Cemetery, and the Theodore Roosevelt Bridge between the Lincoln Memorial and Kennedy Center for the Performing Arts. The last span, the Francis Scott Key Bridge, connects Georgetown and Rosslyn, Virginia.

Its numerous shortcomings notwithstanding, National Airport was prized by members of Congress, government officials, and those having business in Washington. Supreme Court justices, some congresspeople, and a handful of VIPs had their own exclusive parking lot near the terminal's front door. The airport was just across the Potomac, four miles by road from the White House and five miles from Capitol Hill, with convenient direct Metro access.

Despite its reputation for danger, there hadn't been a fatal commercial airliner crash at National Airport for thirty-three years. Some argued that National was safe *because* it was dangerous — that pilots were forced to be extra attentive and cautious around the airport.

The last deadly commercial aviation incident happened on the morning of November 1, 1949, when a World War II surplus P-38 fighter plane flown by a Bolivian air force captain collided with an Eastern Airlines DC-4 arriving from New York City. The Bolivian pilot survived with serious injuries, but the DC-4 broke apart and fell into the Potomac River off Hains Point, killing the fifty-one passengers and four crew members aboard. It was at the time the nation's deadliest commercial aviation disaster.

2:20 P.M.

Robert McKeon, an American Airlines mechanic, stood in an elevated cherry-picker basket and began to hose down the left side of Flight 90 with deicing solution — a pinkish mixture of ethylene glycol antifreeze and water.

Ice is a serious hazard in aviation, widely recognized among pilots. The presence of ice on airfoil surfaces, even in trace amounts, causes turbulence of the air crossing the wing. If the airflow is disrupted too much, the wing will lose the ability to maintain the lift necessary to remain airborne.

FAA regulations prohibited a pilot from flying a plane with snow or ice on the wings. Air Florida's operating manual forbade it, placing responsibility on the pilot to ensure that the wings were free of debris.

Boeing 737s, one of the most common airliners used in commercial aviation, had a well-known tendency for the nose to pitch upward when the wings were glazed with ice or snow. Unless the pilot immediately increased power to the engines, the airplane would stall.

In September 1981, Air Florida chief 737 pilot Jim Marquis wrote about winter flight operations in the company's in-house newsletter for crews. He instructed flight crews to be vigilant for snow or ice accumulation. Marquis advised pilots to have their planes deiced "as late as practical before push-back" from the gate. It might be necessary to be deiced again if a plane was significantly delayed on the ground during heavy freezing precipitation.

Deicing works two ways. The glycol solution is heated to 190 degrees Fahrenheit and sprayed under pressure at a rate of thirty gallons per minute, clearing snow off the plane. Glycol raises the freezing point of water and inhibits the formation of ice on the wing. But the antifreeze effect doesn't last for long.

McKeon had hosed down the left wing and a portion of the fuselage when National Airport's maintenance chief, George Lynch, told Wheaton that the airport wasn't going to reopen until 2:53. Snow was coming down heavily and at that rate would accumulate on the plane within minutes.

"It's best to wait until the last possible minute to deice," Lynch told the captain. Wheaton told McKeon to halt deicing.

Anticipating a rush when the airport reopened, Wheaton asked for deicing at 2:45. McKeon returned with the cherry-picker and sprayed the fuselage and both wings with heated deicing fluid, completing the task at around 3:10.

3:15 P.M.

Seated in front of a bank of windows in the air traffic control tower, Stanley Gromelski looked out at the snowy airfield. A veteran of seventeen years as an air traffic controller, Gromelski was a supervisor responsible for local control — guiding planes at the airport from the gate until takeoff.

Once a plane left the runway and reached four hundred to five hundred feet, responsibility for it was handed over to departure control. Different air traffic controllers took over when a plane reached cruising altitude. This carefully calibrated process of air traffic control ensured that planes remained a safe distance away from one another.

Gromelski told Flight 90 it was cleared to push back from the gate, sixteenth in line for takeoff.

Adams, the senior flight attendant, closed the airliner cabin door and lingered by the open cockpit to chat. As is customary among flight crews, Wheaton and Pettit switched roles for the flight back to Florida, with Pettit assuming the lead as pilot and Wheaton acting as copilot.

Wheaton asked the Air Florida station manager, standing at the end of the open walkway, to visually inspect the plane. Just a light dusting of snow on the left wing, the station manager told him.

They waited for a tug to come over and push the plane back from the gate.

Edward Kovarik of Atlanta, an executive for Southern Railway, flew into Washington for a meeting. He had a window seat in an Eastern Airlines plane waiting for space to open at a gate. Kovarik saw Flight 90 about two hundred feet away, at Gate 12.

An amateur photographer whose hobby was taking pictures of airplanes, between 3:19 and 3:24 Kovarik raised his Cannon AE1 to the window and snapped the shutter.

Ten to fifteen minutes after Flight 90 was deiced, snow was clearly visible along the top of the fuselage.

A tug rolled over and latched on to Flight 90's nose gear to move it away from the gate. The tarmac was slippery with slushy snow and deicing fluid, and the tug's tires spun uselessly. Another tug would have to be summoned, one equipped with chains on the tires.

Wheaton asked the tug driver about using reverse thrusters to push back from the gate. Reverse thrusters are scoops that deploy from the engine cowling and redirect the exhaust forward to slow down the plane when landing.

Reverse thrusters can also be used to push the plane backward, but the tug operator told Wheaton that the use of reverse thrusters at the gate was against American Airlines policy.

In a 1980 bulletin to customers, Boeing warned against using reverse thrusters in wintry conditions because of the risk that snow melted by the hot exhaust would refreeze on the leading edge of the wing. The redirected exhaust could push debris on the wing and cowling forward, possibly blocking a sensor port critical for monitoring the engine. Boeing advised pilots to inspect the wings before takeoff if reverse thrusters were used in snowy or icing conditions.

Nonetheless, Wheaton powered up the engines and deployed the reverse thrusters for thirty to ninety seconds to no avail. The plane wouldn't budge.

A member of the ground crew reported seeing snow and slush blown forward when the reverse thrusters were deployed. He examined each engine and found them all free of debris.

Within minutes another tug, with chains on its tires, easily moved through the slush and pushed the 737 away from the gate.

"Stand by for salute and we'll see ya later," the tug driver told Wheaton, referring to the signal for the plane to proceed to the taxiway.

"Right-o, thanks a lot," Wheaton replied.

As the plane pulled away from the gate, Kelly Duncan

turned to Marilyn Nichols. "Aren't they going to deice us again?" she asked. "We've been sitting here awhile."

Nichols had no answer. The flight attendants took their places in the aisle as Adams recited the familiar preflight safety instructions from the front of the plane. The women gestured to the emergency exits, demonstrated how to work the seat belt buckle, and explained about oxygen masks overhead in event of a rapid depressurization.

Although the plane had inflatable flotation vests stored beneath each seat, passengers were not told how to inflate or wear them. The FAA did not require it unless a flight was fifty or more miles over open water.

Every commercial airliner has two rugged devices, commonly called black boxes, to provide information about the last moments of a flight that ends in disaster. The boxes aren't black but colored a high-visibility orange. They are installed in the tail of a plane, where they are least likely to be destroyed in a crash.

One of the devices is a flight data recorder (FDR), which keeps track of the status of the airplane and the flight. The second device is the cockpit voice recorder (CVR), a four-channel audio system that records the last thirty minutes of communication among the pilots and airplane crew, and between the cockpit crew and air traffic control.

Most of the talk recorded on Flight 90's CVR was related to the aircraft. Important facts were conveyed when Pettit and Wheaton performed the predeparture checklist.

Pettit:	*Cutout?*
Wheaton:	*After start.*
Pettit:	*Electrical?*
Wheaton:	*Generators.*
Pettit:	*Pitot heat?*
Wheaton:	*On.*
Pettit:	*Anti-ice?*
Wheaton:	*Off.*
Pettit:	*APU?*
Wheaton:	*Running.*
Pettit:	*Start levers?*
Wheaton:	*Idle.*

The pilots made a grave error. Perhaps out of habit, accustomed to flying in the warm climate of Florida, the engine anti-ice system was turned off. The anti-ice system prevents the formation of ice on the air intake openings of the engine nacelle, the center of the jet fans in the front of the engine. In this weather, the anti-ice system should have been on.

The CVR also recorded conversations about the weather. "Boy, this is shitty," Pettit said to Wheaton. "It's probably the shittiest snow I've seen."

Pettit pointed out an airport maintenance worker near a Cessna Citation, a midsized business jet. "That Citation over there, that guy's about ankle-deep in it."

The flight attendants, on the other hand, were delighted by the snow.

"I love it out here," Adams said.

"Look at all the tire tracks in the snow," Nichols chimed in.

From an adjacent taxiway, Captain Hall Bond was in the cockpit of a Braniff airliner waiting in line for takeoff. He looked over at Flight 90 and noted snow, and possibly ice, frosting the top of the fuselage from the nose to the tail, as well as the forward surface of the left wing and part of left engine.

"Look at the junk on that plane," Bond told his copilot.

3:45 P.M.

Flight 90 progressed toward the front of the line for take-off, more than a half hour after the plane had been deiced. Pettit and Wheaton bantered about snow on the wings.

"Tell you what, my windshield will be deiced," Pettit said. "Don't know about my wing."

Wheaton reassured the first officer that the snow would be blown off the wings as the plane accelerated down the runway. "Well, all we need is the inside of the wing anyway," he said. "The wingtips are gonna speed up by eighty [knots, about ninety-two miles per hour] anyway. They'll shuck all that other stuff."

After this exchange, the transcript of the CVR audio recording noted the sound of laughter.

Pettit brought up the wings again. "Did they get yours? Can you see your wingtip over there?"

"I got a little on mine," Wheaton said.

"This one's got about a quarter to half an inch on it all the way," Pettit remarked.

Minutes later, Pettit noticed a discrepancy between two cockpit instruments and brought it to Wheaton's attention.

"See this difference in that left engine and right one?" Pettit asked.

"Yeah," was the only response.

"I don't know why that's different."

The crew of Flight 90 didn't know it, but ice had blocked an intake port on an engine nacelle, possibly when the reverse thrusters were deployed. The intake port is for a system to measure the engine pressure ratio (EPR). By measuring the air pressure in front of and behind the engine, the system calculates the thrust being produced by the engine. With one port blocked, an instrument displayed a falsely elevated pressure. The engine wasn't producing as much thrust as the pilots were led to believe.

Pettit searched for an explanation, and thought the disparity might have been caused by hot exhaust from the jet in front of them going into their right engine. "That must be it," he said to himself. An element of uncertainty remained in his tone. "It was doing that in the chocks [at the gate] awhile ago but, uh . . ." His voice trailed off.

3:51 P.M.

Flight 90 was slowly moving up the line, now behind a New York Air DC-9, known by its air traffic control sign as Apple.

"We still fourth?" Nichols asked the cockpit over the plane's phone.

"Yeah" Pettit told her. "We're getting there. We used to be seventh."

Pettit pulled his 737 up close to the DC-9 so the jet's hot exhaust might melt the snow on his wings and was frustrated when the plane rolled away.

"Don't do that, Apple, I need the other wing done," Wheaton joked.

If anything, trying to melt snow on the wings with hot engine exhaust is likely detrimental. With the frigid air temperature, melted snow would just refreeze as ice.

Pettit bemoaned the futility of deicing planes during a snowstorm. "Boy, this is a losing battle here on trying to deice those things," he said. "It gives you a false sense of security."

"It satisfies the feds," Wheaton said.

It had been forty minutes since Flight 90 was deiced. If they returned to the terminal for deicing, the plane would lose its place in line and be delayed even further.

Wheaton came up with the clever idea of making planes pass between a gauntlet of deicing trucks just before going onto the runway.

"Yeah, and you taxi through kinda like a car wash or something," Pettit said.

"Hit that thing with about eight billion gallons of glycol," Wheaton added.

"Boy, I bet all the schoolkids are just crapping their pants here," Pettit said. "It's fun for them. No school tomorrow. Yahoo!"

3:59 P.M.

Flight 90 was ready to go at the end of Runway 38, waiting for an arriving TWA plane to roll onto the taxiway and get out of the way.

The CVR captured the pilots discussing the takeoff.

"Slushy runway," Pettit said. "Do you want me to do anything special for this or just go for it?"

"Unless you got anything special you'd like to do," Wheaton replied.

"Unless just take off the nose wheel early like a soft field takeoff or something," Pettit said. "I'll just take the nose wheel off and then we'll let it fly off. Be out the three two six, climbing to five. I'll pull it back to about one point five five, supposed to be one six depending on how scared we are."

At 3:59:24, Pettit was given the final go-ahead.

"Palm Ninety, cleared for takeoff," Gromelski said from the air traffic control tower.

"Palm Ninety, cleared for takeoff," Pettit acknowledged.

"No delay on departure, if you will," Gromelski said. "Traffic's two and a half [miles] out for the runway."

Gromelski was informing Pettit that another plane — Eastern Flight 1451 — was cleared to land on Runway 36. The distance between the planes was unusually close. FAA regulations required a distance of at least three miles between planes during takeoff or landings.

Pettit may have felt pressure to get off the ground quickly. Data indicates that the distance between Flight 90 and Eastern Flight 1451 was less than a mile, both planes on Runway

36 at the same time. Pettit never expressed concern that a plane was closing in behind them.

"Ladies and gentlemen, we have just been cleared for takeoff," Pettit said over the public address system. "Flight attendants, please be seated."

Adams took her seat in the front galley, near the cockpit, where the senior flight attendant usually sits. Junior attendants are supposed to sit next to the aft galley. But today was different. Nichols wanted to spend time with her friend and sat with Adams up front, leaving Duncan sitting by herself in back.

Flight 90 rolled down Runway 36, slowly gaining speed. But the engines were only producing 80 percent as much thrust as they were supposed to. As the plane accelerated, Pettit recognized that something was wrong. He drew Wheaton's attention to the engine pressure ratio reading while the captain kept track of their speed.

"That doesn't seem right, does it?" Pettit said. "Ah, that's not right."

"Yes it is," Wheaton replied. "There's eighty [knots]."

"Naw, I don't think that's right," Pettit said. "Ah, maybe it is."

"A hundred and twenty," Wheaton said.

"I don't know," Pettit said.

The plane was approaching V_1, the takeoff decision speed of 138 knots, the last chance to safely abort the takeoff. This is the moment, if there are any concerns or doubts, to kill the throttle. Only the captain can abort a takeoff. Wheaton said nothing.

In the aft galley, Duncan could tell that the plane wasn't going as fast as usual. Ordinarily, the engines were so deafeningly loud that she covered her ears. But not today.

As Flight 90 shambled down the runway, in her mind Duncan willed the plane off the ground.

Get this baby in the air, she thought. *Get this baby in the air.*

Flight 90 traveled fifty-two hundred feet down Runway 36, about thirteen hundred feet more than normal for a 737, and listlessly rose into the air.

The stick shaker alarm began almost as soon as the plane left the ground, warning that the aircraft was about to stall and lose its aerodynamic lift. The correct action would be to push the throttle, the equivalent of flooring it, to gain speed. Pilots are instructed not to push engines to their limits because of the risk of costly damage. But given the choice between human lives and maintenance costs, the decision should have been obvious.

Pettit never pushed the throttle. The wings began buffeting as they lost grip of the low pressure keeping the aircraft aloft, causing the plane to shudder violently.

Wheaton urged Pettit to gain altitude without tipping into a stall. "Forward, forward," he yelled. "Easy. We only want five hundred. Come on, forward. Forward. Just barely climb."

Air Florida 90 was airborne for half a mile and reached a maximum altitude of 352 feet — less than the height of the Washington Monument in the distance — then stalled and plummeted at 150 miles per hour toward the two hundred vehicles lined up on the 14th Street Bridge.

The final words captured on Air Florida 90's cockpit voice recorder:

Pettit: *We're going down, Larry.*
Wheaton: *I know it.*

4:01 P.M.

Navigating a six-ton truck in city traffic isn't easy. The heavy snowfall only made driving more challenging for Albert Jackson, behind the wheel of a Ford boom truck — a flatbed mounted with a twenty-foot crane.

Jackson and Marion Grant Jr., employees of P&P Construction, were returning to the company's Rockville headquarters after delivering a load of concrete block to a construction site in Crystal City. The men were in high spirits despite the foul weather. The workday was done, and they were headed home.

Ordinarily, Jackson would have taken the shortest route to Rockville — the George Washington Memorial Parkway to the I-495 Beltway, and then north on I-270 toward Frederick. But traffic on the parkway was moving at a crawl, and the Beltway would only be worse. Jackson suggested they stay on I-395 and go straight through the District of Columbia.

As they approached the 14th Street Bridge in the far-right-hand lane, traffic was stop and go. About a hundred feet from the Virginia end of the bridge, the truck's progress was stalled by a stranded car in the lane ahead. Jackson tapped the left-turn signal and eased the truck over two lanes to the far-left-hand lane of I-395.

Grant heard a rumbling that grew increasingly louder, like a freight train bearing down on them.

"You hear that?" he asked Jackson.

The men looked around and saw nothing but furiously billowing snow.

A few car lengths behind them, Lloyd Shelton was driving his 1978 Plymouth Arrow. A twenty-three-year-old navy ensign from Bowling Green, Ohio, Shelton was temporarily assigned to the Pentagon until flight navigation training began in June. When federal employees were released early, his was among the mass of vehicles leaving the Pentagon parking lots at the same time.

This blizzard was nothing compared with the snow conditions Shelton was used to in northeastern Ohio, but in Washington it was enough to snarl his six-mile commute home.

Shelton heard a whir that swelled into a deafening roar.

Suddenly, the stark white belly of an impossibly large jetliner dropping from the sky emerged from the snowy haze. Nose up slightly, wings angled to the left, the plane seemed to fall from nowhere.

From Shelton's perspective, it appeared the plane was going to land directly on him. Surrounded on all sides by other cars, he was trapped. There was no time to react.

The thundering roar of jet engines drowned out Shelton's scream. Gripping the steering wheel, he watched the massive jetliner skid across three lanes of traffic, crushing several cars and shearing the tops off others, tossing them around like toys.

Skimming inches over the hood of Shelton's car, the tip of the left wing grazed his windshield, smashing a hole in the glass and ripping off the right windshield wiper. The windshield exploded, blasting the car's interior with shards of glass. Shelton cut his lip.

Jackson and Grant were slammed from the side as the plane's right wing struck the P&P Construction truck's crane, snapping it in half. The crane tore into the wing's leading-edge slat, tipping the vehicle at a perilous angle toward the water. Dangling to the left, the damaged crane propped the truck up like a kickstand, preventing it from toppling off the bridge into the Potomac.

The midsection of the plane struck the bridge sidewall, knocking out 41 feet of concrete and pulling down 137 feet of barrier railing. Instantly, the airframe shattered into pieces. The airliner's nose and cockpit punched through the ice and plunged into the Potomac between the northbound and HOV spans of I-395, sinking into twenty-five feet of water, followed by the fragmented fuselage. The tail section, separated from the rest of the fuselage, tumbled over the cars on the bridge and dropped into the water.

In the plane's wake, sheets of ice fell from the sky.

David Mastric, sixteen years old, was shoveling snow from the front walk of his next-door neighbor on North Upshur

Street in Arlington. His family lived on a pleasant, settled cul-de-sac with ancient oaks and maple trees.

On a day like this, the snow muted sound to softness, except for the periodic rumble of a flight leaving National Airport. Living less than a mile from the flight path over the Potomac River, residents of this community were accustomed to noise from the airport blending into the background.

Still grounded by his strict military father for being caught with $5 worth of pot the previous June, the only time Mastric was allowed out of his bedroom at home was to do chores. He spent most of the afternoon shoveling the sidewalk in front of the family home and, at his father's insistence, the walk of the woman who lived next door.

Shortly after 4:00 P.M., Mastric heard the familiar low guttural moan of an airliner in the distance. And then the noise suddenly ceased. Stark silence. Mastric stopped shoveling and scanned the gray sky over the homes to the northeast. Nothing. After a few moments, he picked up the shovel and resumed clearing the sidewalk.

Stunned, Shelton tried to make sense of what had just happened. At first, he thought his windshield had shattered because of the loud noise. He unfastened his seat belt and stepped out. Cars in front of him were crumpled and tossed around the bridge.

He looked out over the water and saw wreckage of an airliner. Scattered amid chunks of ice were luggage, clothing, shoes, seat cushions, pieces of metal and plastic, and a white naval officer's hat. Bodies were visible beneath the surface of the water. Shelton turned away. The sight was too disturbing.

He walked around on the bridge in a daze, unsure of what to do. A young woman who was in a car ahead of him and to the left approached Shelton and asked if he had any cloth material that could be used as bandages. A passenger in her car was injured and bleeding heavily from the head. Shelton didn't understand her question, so she repeated herself. He reached into his back seat and gave her T-shirts from his laundry.

One driver exited his car, looked over the side of the bridge at the scattered pieces of an airliner, and began to cry. A woman got out of her car, looked around, and fainted.

In the P&P Construction truck up ahead, Grant climbed over the driver's seat and dropped six feet through the open door to the ground. Trembling, he looked around at the unbelievable damage.

Behind their truck was a Mustang with a partially flattened roof, spun sideways on the bridge deck. A woman who had been riding in the Mustang, apparently uninjured, screamed for help. Grant looked inside her car and saw that the driver's head was crushed.

Another car had a tire track across the roof. Grant saw the immobile legs of the driver, his feet resting on the pedals. From another car, he heard somebody strangling on their own blood.

There were so many people trapped in mangled vehicles. So many injured people. Grant walked around to see if he could do anything to help.

He thought about how close he and Jackson had been to death. If the plane had been a few inches lower, they would have been killed. Had Jackson not moved to the far-left-hand lane, the truck would have been directly in the plane's path.

This lane or that, one route or another. A fraction of a second faster or slower was the difference between life and death. Was it luck, or something else?

Looking out to the dark hole in the field of broken ice, Grant saw a hand reach out from the water.

part three

The Awakening

Joe Stiley regained consciousness in darkness, still belted in his seat. Cold water was lapping at his chin and rising fast. He took a deep breath to fill his lungs. The fuselage slowly settled in the water and rested in the muck at the bottom of the Potomac River.

Long-dormant water survival training from his navy days stirred into action. *Stay in control,* he said to himself. As the wreckage sank, he made a mental checklist:

> *Get the seat belt*
> *Get Nikki*
> *Go aft — if there's a safe way out, it's probably to the rear*

His legs painfully wedged beneath the seat in front of him, Stiley tugged against sharp metal digging into his shins to free himself. Reaching over to Felch, he found that she had already unfastened her seat belt and pulled her legs from twisted metal.

Unable to communicate underwater, they clumsily pushed each other through the jumble of debris, clambering over the lifeless bodies of the two students Stiley had been talking with only minutes earlier, and floated toward the surface. He was worried they might be trapped beneath ice, and about how to tell Felch to find an air bubble.

Flight attendant Kelly Duncan was disoriented but strangely tranquil, bathed in white light. She could see herself, as though watching a movie.

This is what dying is like, Duncan thought to herself. *It would be so easy to let go and slip away.*

No. I'm not really ready to die.

Frigid water slapped her awake. Duncan's seat was hardly damaged. She reached down to unfasten her seat belt and swim toward sunlight where the plane had split in front of her.

Felch and Stiley surfaced near a section of the fuselage jutting out from a large hole in the ice. They drifted over to the jagged wreckage and held on to keep their heads above water. Pieces of yellow-orange foam that Stiley recognized as insulation from the airliner wall floated by.

They thought they were alone, the only survivors.

Duncan surfaced around fifteen feet away from the others. She looked at the distance to the riverbank, across the expansive white tabletop of ice, and initially thought she could make it to shore. Before undertaking the effort, she swam to the shredded section of fuselage to gather herself. But once she reached the wreckage and had a better sense on her predicament, she realized that she never would have made it. She probably would have died trying to get across or under the ice. Duncan had no choice but stay put and wait to be rescued.

Bert Hamilton never panicked. Once on the surface, separated from the others, he was able to keep his upper body out of the water by standing on a cable pulled taut in the debris. Hamilton felt oddly calm, his attention irrationally focused on his left foot. His shoe had slipped off, and he was concerned that his foot would get cold. The most important thing in the world was putting his left shoe back on his foot.

He wasn't sure what happened. *It couldn't have been a plane crash*, he thought. *People don't survive a plane crash, and I'm still alive.*

For a few moments, it was hauntingly quiet, with all sound muffled by the snow. A mist of vapor hung over the water. The air was heavy with the odor of jet fuel from the fully loaded plane, posing an uncertain risk of fire or explosion. Jet fuel, essentially kerosene, is toxic to humans. Ingestion of jet fuel poses as much risk to the survivors as drowning.

A woman's shriek pierced the silence. "My baby! My baby! Help me find my baby!"

Priscilla Tirado was frantically treading in circles in open water, several feet away from the others. "Somebody please help me find my baby!" she screamed.

Nikki Felch held on to the fuselage and reached her right arm out to Tirado. Her hand dangled down uselessly from her shattered wrist. She was worried that Tirado would pull her hand off. Stiley found a length of broken plastic and held it out for Tirado to grasp.

Tirado scrambled through the water and grabbed Stiley's necktie with both hands, pulling him underwater. "My baby," she wailed. "Help me find my baby."

"Stop it, let go of his tie," Felch said. "You'll make him drown."

"Settle down and we'll help you find your baby," Stiley said. He thought maybe she'd come up with a baby and it had slipped out of her arms and might be floating nearby. Tirado kept a grip on his belt.

Stiley looked around at their dismal surroundings. They were a hundred feet from the riverbank, separated by an expanse of ice several inches thick. The shore might as well have been miles away.

His body was racked with pain. Bones were fractured — the tibia and fibula of the left lower leg, the right lower leg, bones in his right hand, ribs. More than sixty fractures in all.

Stiley reflected on how drastically things changed in an instant. One moment he's sitting in a warm airliner cabin, the next moment he's dunked in freezing water.

I survived a plane crash, Stiley thought to himself. *Now I'm going to freeze to death.*

The water of the Potomac River was just above freezing at thirty-four degrees Fahrenheit. The air was twenty-four degrees, with a gentle ten-mile-an-hour wind from the south that produced a chill factor in the teens.

Immersed in excruciatingly cold water, the crash survivors were held in a relentless icy grip. The frigid water stung with a chill that penetrated to the bone, like millions of crystalline needles piercing the skin.

A person submerged in water loses body heat twenty-five times faster than on dry land. Aside from drowning, the greatest risk of cold-water immersion is hypothermia, a body core temperature of ninety-five degrees or lower. The immediate reaction to cold-water immersion is typically hyperventilation, breathing at a rate five or more times faster than normal, leading to a loss of carbon dioxide that can cause muscle spasms and contribute to a sense of panic.

When a body is exposed to an extremely cold environment, superficial blood vessels in the skin constrict to reduce heat loss. Lacking circulating blood, the skin turns pale and loses sensation. Muscles begin an involuntary rapid twitch, shivering, to generate more heat. The result of shivering is often the opposite in the water, however, where heat is lost faster if a person is physically active.

As the body core temperature drops, blood is shunted away from the extremities to preserve heat and circulation for the vital organs — the heart and brain. The extremities become less responsive, beginning with the hands and feet and extending to the larger muscles as the body cools. Using the arms and legs becomes increasingly difficult. Judgment and cognition decline.

If hypothermia progresses, nerves stop effectively conducting impulses. Reflexes are diminished, and the risk of the heartbeat developing into fatal ventricular fibrillation rises dramatically. Shivering stops. A person will become increasingly lethargic and confused, eventually slipping into unconsciousness.

With a core body temperature of ninety degrees Fahrenheit or below, cardiac output declines as a person's blood pressure drops and the heart rate slows down. The lungs become congested. In the absence of rapid treatment and rewarming, the person will ultimately die.

Under the conditions faced by the victims of Flight 90, the risk of death is about 50 percent within fifteen minutes. Sixty minutes is not survivable.

"Palm Ninety, Departure."

"Palm Ninety, Departure."

By the time Flight 90 reached five hundred feet in altitude, the plane should have appeared on the departure radar with detailed transponder information. The pilot should have checked in with the departure air traffic controller. Neither of those things happened.

As the seconds ticked by, anxious air traffic controllers waited for another sweep of the radar. Still nothing.

Stanley Gromelski had watched Flight 90 roll past the tower but was unable to see the end of the runway. Visibility was reduced to a quarter mile. He wasn't sure whether Flight 90 had rejected the takeoff and was sitting at the end of the runway or had experienced a problem in the cockpit — or if something else altogether was wrong.

The controller asked an arriving flight to taxi to the end of Runway 36 and see if anything was visible. Minutes later the pilot of the arriving plane reported seeing tire tracks nearly to the end of the runway. And the overrun was completely blown clear of snow. There were two sets of tire tracks, indicating that the nose of the plane was off the ground. Beyond that was an impenetrable haze of flurries.

A supervisor picked up a phone and called the Twin Bridges Marriott, a five-story motel across I-395 from the Pentagon at the Virginia end of the 14th Street Bridge. Reed Pullan, the twenty-nine-year-old manager on duty who answered the phone, was asked to go see if a jetliner had crashed.

Pullan put the caller on hold, took the elevator to the fifth floor, and walked to an empty guest room at the end of the corridor. He peered out the window through billowing snow. There was no smoke, no flames, no airplane debris. Pullan picked up the phone and pressed the blinking button.

"There's no airplane crash," he reported back. "A truck is tipped over on the bridge and traffic is backed up, but I don't see a crashed airplane."

Mike Patterson inched across the 14th Street Bridge toward Washington in his car, with Pentagon colleagues Aldo De La Cruz and Steve Raynes along for the ride. Suddenly, the music they were listening to was overwhelmed by the roar of jet engines.

The howling engine was earsplitting, like the F-4 Phantom fighter jets De La Cruz heard when he and his friends sat at the end of the runway at the air force base in Texas as kids. Looking out the window to the left, De La Cruz noticed smoke rising from the water between the bridges.

"Steve, something's not right," he said to Raynes, sitting in front of him. "Let me out."

Raynes and De La Cruz got out of Patterson's car and looked around at the incomprehensible scene of havoc. Cars were mangled and crushed, scattered around the bridge deck. They hurried from car to car, looking for injured victims they could help.

Behind them, a crane truck was nearly toppled off the bridge. Tossed sideways on the road, a car was crushed down to the level of the seats, a tire track running across the roof. A man screamed from within a crumpled black Renault. Without tools to pry open the cars, Raynes and De La Cruz could be of no help.

Next to the Renault was a car with the top peeled off.

The driver, an air force officer, was in the driver's seat with his foot on the brake and his gloved hands on the steering wheel. The top of the car, and the driver's head, were cut off as neatly as if it were done by a gigantic knife.

De La Cruz saw people clinging onto a jagged piece of fuselage out in the water, in a clearing in the ice. They were screaming.

These people in the cars are going to get help, he reasoned. *I need to go to the water's edge and see what I can do to help the people in the water.*

De La Cruz gestured to a car with a distinctive citizen's band (CB) radio antenna. "Get on channel nine," he told airman Steve Raynes. "Call for help."

Wearing just a long-sleeved shirt and athletic shoes — dressed for the racquetball court, not a winter rescue — he ran down the bridge to the riverside where people had begun to congregate.

Roger Olian kept an eye on his Datsun pickup truck's gas gauge, which was getting worryingly close to empty. He desperately needed to get off the bridge, off I-395 onto a local street and to a gas station. Traffic was working against him, not moving at all.

"Aw jeez, this is all I need," he muttered.

Looking up from his dashboard, Olian saw the driver of the car ahead of him running to his truck. He rolled down his window to hear what the man had to say.

"Did you see that?" he said to Olian. "A plane just cashed into the river. I'm afraid it's going to blow up."

Olian thought the man had lost his mind. He hadn't seen or heard anything.

"If you think it's going to blow up, maybe you should get out of here," Olian said.

Then Olian noticed people acting strangely, a flurry of activity on the bridge. People were getting out of their cars and running back and forth, like the random movement caused by poking an anthill.

Olian pulled his truck over, got out, and leaned over the bridge wall. He saw people in the water, hanging on to debris. He turned off his truck and broke into a sprint down the bridge to the riverside.

Several cars behind Olian, farther back on the outbound 14th Street Bridge, a father and son shared the back seat of a station wagon. Ordinarily, Martin Leonard "Lenny" Skutnik III would drive his own car to work, but with today's weather he'd decided to join his dad's carpool and leave his at home.

Skutnik had held a series of menial jobs over the years; housepainter, meat packer, hamburger cook. He finally took the advice of his father, Martin L. Skutnik Jr., who worked in the budget office of the Department of Health and Human Services, and applied for a federal civil service job.

At twenty-eight years of age, the younger Skutnik earned $14,000 a year as a clerk in the Congressional Budget Office. He served as a general go-fer, delivering mail, running the photocopier, and doing whatever else needed to be done. It was a job that came with the privilege of learning the inner workings of Congress and paid enough to sustain a decent life for a family with two young children in Lorton, Virginia.

Somebody came up to the carpool, tapped on the window, and asked whether they had any rope. The Skutnik men got out of the station wagon and saw people looking out over the Potomac. Lenny looked through the gloomy mist over the water, unable to see what was drawing so much attention.

A woman's voice punctured the slashing snow. "Help me! Please help me!"

The hair on Lenny's neck stood on end. Somebody was in the water. He ran to the Virginia end of the bridge, toward where a small group of people were gathering at the riverside.

By the time Olian reached the low bluff at the edge of the Potomac, De La Cruz and others had tried to devise ways to rescue the people in the water. Somebody suggested breaking off a tree branch. What good would that do? They were too far out. What about a spare tire? Would a spare tire float?

Several motorists brought jumper cables from their trunks. Tied together, the jumper cables formed a sort of lifeline. But it was far too heavy to throw out to survivors, and too short to reach them.

Olian ran through the crowd and slid on his back down the embankment to the river. He broke through the ice, stepping into the water.

"You can't go out there," somebody said from the riverbank. "You'll freeze to death."

"I can't stand here and watch them die," he yelled back.

"Take this," a bystander said, holding out the jumper cables.

Olian took the improvised lifeline, tied it around his waist, and walked into the water. He thought the Potomac River was shallow enough that he might be able to wade out to the survivors, but the steeply sloped bottom quickly led Olian into deep water, so cold it stung like an electric shock.

4:05 P.M.

Evelyne "Evie" White was a volunteer with Radio Emergency Associated Communications Team (REACT), a nationwide network providing two-way radio communication during emergencies and special events. REACT was an essential resource to motorists in need of assistance and communities struck by natural disasters.

At home in Fairfax, Virginia, with the radio scanner running in the background as always, White heard a call on channel nine, the citizen's band emergency frequency: *A plane crashed into the 14th Street Bridge. People are injured.*

White picked up her phone and dialed the Arlington County Emergency Communications Center, the centralized office for police, fire, and emergency medical services. It had been a very busy day because of the snowstorm, all the lines lit up with fender-benders and people in need of assistance. Communications tech Richard Singer had just been rotated off the police dispatch desk for his four-hour shift taking phone calls.

White identified herself as a REACT volunteer. It wasn't uncommon for REACT volunteers to call about an incident, but this one was out of the ordinary. White told Singer that a 747 had crashed into the 14th Street Bridge.

That doesn't sound right, Singer thought. *Boeing 747s can't land at National Airport.*

Singer was uncertain about the call. It was so unusual, so spectacular. He turned to Arlington police chief William "Smokey" Stover, behind him in the room, for guidance. "Check it out," Stover said.

Singer dialed the direct line to National's air traffic control tower. "Do you have any aircraft missing?" he asked. "We had a report of a plane hitting the 14th Street Bridge."

"Send everything you have," an air traffic control supervisor said.

"A plane is missing?" Singer asked.

"Just send everybody," he was told.

Singer stared at the blinking green cursor on the dispatch system monitor in front of him. Once entered into the system, information would be sent to the police and fire/EMS dispatch desks and set the county's emergency response in motion. He typed all he knew about the nature of the incident — "PLANE CRASH — 14TH STREET BRIDGE" — and hit the TRANSMIT button.

In the alarm room of National Airport's fire station, a deputy fire chief had been monitoring air traffic control radio chatter about Flight 90. He ordered two fire/crash trucks to the end of Runway 36 and a fire/crash truck and ambulance to head north on the George Washington Memorial Parkway.

Seconds later, the airport tower officially notified the fire station, triggering alarms and a clock that logged the time. Emergency vehicles were already on the way.

Olian pulled the jumper cables tied around his waist and was swiftly in water over his head. He was still wearing his work clothes, including parka, wool cap, and steel-toed boots, which made swimming extremely difficult. Jet fuel floated on the water, leaving a nauseating oily residue in Olian's mouth when he spit it out.

Bystanders on the riverbank lengthened the improvised tether with whatever they could scrounge from nearby vehicles — an extension cord, clothesline, scarves, a belt. One woman contributed her pantyhose. Link by link, the lifeline grew longer.

The wreckage looked so far away in the water. Olian considered how to make his way there. Ice was broken into large slabs several inches thick that left no room to navigate in between. He couldn't push them out of the way. Swimming under a floe was terrifying. Olian feared being trapped beneath the ice or tangled on underwater debris.

People on shore shouted advice to him. "Get up on the ice," somebody yelled.

"Great idea," Olian said under his breath, "but somebody left the handles off the ice."

Olian gripped the ice with numb hands, lifted himself up, and slipped off back into the water. Over and over, he grappled to gain a foothold and then dunked back into the water until finally he was able to roll onto an ice floe. Then he slowly crept across, pulling the lifeline behind him, and slid back into the water.

Standing chest-deep in frigid water, Bert Hamilton looked up to the HOV bridge high overhead. A group of passengers filed out of a WMATA bus and lined up on the railing, peering down over the sidewall.

"Get help, get boats," he yelled at them. "Get us out of here."

The group filed back onto the bus without responding.

My God, nobody knows we're here, Hamilton thought to himself.

Joe Stiley discovered a sixth survivor holding on to the other side of the wreckage, within sight of him but not the others. The sixth, bank examiner Arland Williams, could barely keep his head above water. The metal framework of his seat was twisted. He was trapped in tangled debris.

"I can't get out," Williams told Stiley. "I can't reach my seat belt."

Stiley slid his hand under the fuselage to see if he could touch Williams. All he felt was cold metal.

"Please help us," Duncan screamed. "We're going to die."

Airports serving regularly scheduled passenger air carriers were required by the FAA to have an Aircraft Rescue and Fire Fighting (ARFF) station for aviation incidents on or near the premises. If a plane went down between airports, the emergency response would depend on whatever municipal, county, or state resources could be mustered.

For aviation incidents in the vicinity of National Airport, the FAA relied on several governmental bodies that the agency had no control over.

Many jurisdictions had learned from natural or manmade disasters and formed pacts, called mutual aid agreements, to assist one another with incidents with the potential for large numbers of casualties that could overwhelm local fire and rescue capabilities.

Within a well-managed jurisdiction, various agencies — police, fire/EMS, emergency operations — periodically conduct exercises together and work through simulated disasters. Sometimes these drills are held by a group of people around a table in a room, so-called tabletop exercises, or involve equipment in the field with mannequins or volunteers filling in as victims.

These exercises are helpful for testing mutual aid agreements by identifying shortfalls, communications issues, gaps in resources, and other potential problems before they arise in the middle of a crisis.

Among police and fire departments in the capital region, mutual aid agreements were little more than lists of phone numbers. There was not a strong tradition of cooperation or coordination among the agencies in the counties, towns, and states adjacent to the District of Columbia.

Washington-area fire departments tended to operate like fiefdoms: loyal to a chief and protective of territory. Individual fire departments routinely practiced skills in simulated exercises as a part of ongoing training, but less often with their counterparts from other jurisdictions. Several fire departments in the Virginia suburbs formed the Northern Virginia Dispatch System, which allowed for the closest vehicle to respond to a call regardless of the jurisdiction.

But any professional courtesies ended at the Potomac River. A driver of a DC fire engine that wandered into Arlington, or vice versa, was likely to receive a severe dressing-down following an irate phone call from a fire chief across the river.

The Metropolitan Washington Council of Governments (COG) is an organization established in 1957 to address regional issues affecting the District of Columbia and neighboring jurisdictions, such as transportation and natural resources. The organization includes representation from DC and twenty-five counties and municipalities.

COG had been encouraging interagency cooperation and regional disaster planning since the 1970s, without much success. The organization facilitated the framework of a mutual aid agreement between Maryland and Virginia in 1973, but nothing further was done to flesh out details of how things like incident command and communications would work in practice.

The organization was instrumental in the creation of the Police Mutual Aid Radio System (PMARS), a network accessible by nineteen Washington-area law enforcement agencies, and the corresponding Fire Mutual Aid Radio System (FMARS), with eleven participating area fire departments. PMARS and FMARS had their limitations. The systems could only be used by radios in dispatch centers or in vehicles equipped with radios capable of receiving the frequency, not by the handheld radios used by first responders. For the most part, each department could only communicate with its own people.

In May 1981, the City of Alexandria held a mock disaster involving two hundred simulated injured passengers on an underground train. Because of shortages of equipment and personnel, it took more than five hours to evacuate all the casualties — unacceptably slow, and deadly in an incident involving fire or smoke.

The DC Fire Department conducted several exercises with the WMATA. Shortly after Metrorail became operational, the fire department held a mock disaster involving a subway tunnel fire. No fire was actually set in the tunnel, but the practice revealed the dicey situation firefighters would face if it were real. The breathing apparatus used by the department supplied thirty minutes of air — not enough to walk into a smoky fifteen-hundred-foot tunnel, work on extinguishing a fire, and walk out alive.

Subsequently, the department purchased updated breathing apparatuses capable of providing an hour of air — thirty of them for the entire workforce.

Within the District of Columbia, the police and fire departments never conducted a disaster exercise together. A mock disaster drill involving multiple jurisdictions and agencies had never been held in the region.

Officials were about to find out how well the disaster system worked.

Others were monitoring the citizen's band radio chatter. Betty Mosley, a REACT volunteer in Prince George's County, Maryland, relayed information about the 14th Street Bridge crash to Dan Rosenson at WMAL, an all-talk FM radio station. Ordinarily flying a Cessna 172 to report on rush-hour traffic as "Captain Dan the Traffic Man," Rosenson was grounded because of the weather.

Rosenson, a member of the REACT network, kept a radio base station in the WMAL newsroom. Mosley's early notification helped WMAL break the news about Flight 90 to its listeners.

A former firefighter and inveterate news hound, Dave Statter had his police/fire radio scanner on out of habit in his rented Pentagon City condo. He had nothing else going on during a snowy afternoon.

Statter was between jobs, having been fired as the traffic reporter for KIX-106 in Alexandria in a disagreement with management about the safety of the station's traffic plane. An electronic sign beneath the wings, which flashed a sponsor's message, created too much drag. One hot afternoon, the Cessna 172 barely cleared the trees at the end of the runway. Statter demanded the sign's removal, which didn't sit well with the sponsor, the ad agency, or his bosses at KIX-106. The sign remained. He didn't.

A friend at WTOP, an all-news FM station, put Statter's

name in for a position as weekend traffic reporter. His hopes were pinned on an interview at the station on Friday, January 15.

Statter's scanner stopped on the channel used by National Airport's fire department and picked up talk about a plane crash near the 14th Street Bridge. On the phone at the time, he only heard part of the transmission. His attention piqued, Statter turned up the volume on the scanner and listened closely.

He called the WTOP newsroom and tried to explain himself to a skeptical assignment desk editor. "Look, you don't know me, but there's been a plane crash on the 14th Street Bridge," he said. "Let me see if I can get up there. I'm not far away."

Statter grabbed his binoculars and got in his car. He slowly wended through Pentagon City and Crystal City, taking side streets and alleys to avoid busy roads, driving as close to the 14th Street Bridge as he could.

4:06 P.M.

The Arlington County Fire Department dispatched three fire engines, two trucks, two medic units, and a battalion chief — the highest-ranking officer on duty. Vehicles from three fire stations took different routes toward the Potomac on snowy streets crammed with rush-hour traffic.

It was Sergeant Kenneth Madden's responsibility to make sure that all Arlington County Police Department vehicles had chains on their tires and were ready for the evening shift. He was in the police garage signing off on paperwork when he heard an exchange over the radio.

"Scout 52," the dispatcher said.

"Scout 52, go ahead," came the reply.

"Check the 14th Street Bridge for a plane down."

"Ten-four."

A plane down? Madden grabbed the phone and called the communications office.

"Tell me about this last call, the plane down," he said. "Is it a traffic plane? A private plane?"

"No, an airliner dropped off the radar," the dispatcher told him.

Madden knew that the prisoner transport van in the parking lot was equipped with chains. He grabbed the keys and drove toward the 14th Street Bridge.

Reed Pullan was aware that there had been a plane crash by the time he returned to the front desk of the Twin Bridges Marriott. The hotel's switchboard lit up with calls from radio stations wanting an eyewitness report, a comment, anything about the crash of Flight 90. He had little to say, but still managed to have his uninformed comments used on the air.

Pullan phoned the hotel's housekeeper and told her to make sure the public bathrooms were clean and stocked. Then he called the kitchen to have the staff brew fresh coffee.

It was going to be a busy evening.

4:07 P.M.

Steve Souder's workday had begun at 3:00 A.M., when the DC Fire Department emergency communications center called him in early for his shift as dispatcher. Plan E had been implemented because of the Upshur clinic fire, rallying more manpower for the department.

Souder's voice had been a reliable presence for the fire department since his first shift as a dispatcher on April 4, 1968, when evening fires erupted in Washington during the unrest after the assassination of Martin Luther King Jr. His gravelly baritone projected a sense of order and authority, earning him the respect of his peers.

Making his way to work in the predawn darkness, Souder drove from his Gaithersburg home down I-270 around the Washington Beltway to Georgia Avenue toward the emergency communications office on the grounds of Howard University.

Along the way, out of professional curiosity, Souder took a brief detour to Upshur Street. He drove around the block, glad not to be standing in the bitter cold facing down a raging, fully involved structure fire.

The emergency communications office remained busy following Souder's arrival. There had been no major incidents other than the Upshur clinic fire, but the weather had produced a seemingly nonstop series of calls about traffic accidents, broken pipes, flooded basements, and medical events requiring ambulances.

After twelve hours on dispatch, Souder stepped back

from the microphone. Outside, snow was falling at a furi-
ous rate. He decided to remain at work awhile, waiting until
6:00 or 7:00 P.M. and making the drive home to Montgomery County once traffic had settled down.

An old friend, battalion chief McEldon Fleming, entered
the emergency communications office. Fleming was the fire
department's Metro liaison officer, the point of contact for
all things related to the WMATA.

"You hungry?" Fleming asked.

"Man, I haven't eaten all day," Souder said.

Fleming drove Souder in his red Suburban to a nearby
Roy Rogers to get hamburgers. The battalion chief was
going to eat his burger on the way home to Wheaton, while
Souder would have his back at the office.

With his hamburger in a paper bag, Souder stepped
into the emergency communications center and found staff
in chaos. The first phone call about Flight 90 had come
through its switchboard: "Did you have a crazy report of a
plane hitting the 14th Street Bridge?" the caller asked, offering no other information.

Another call from a radio telephone relayed information broadcast over the citizen's band. "We just received
word over the CB radio that there's been an airplane crash
into the 14th Street Bridge," the unnamed caller said.
"They're calling for ropes, ladders, and everything else.
And blankets."

"The 14th Street Bridge?" the dispatcher asked.

"That's the information I have," the caller said. "Somebody said a 727 crashed."

"A 727," the dispatcher repeated.

"That's correct," the caller said. "There are several cars taken out on the bridge."

A third call reported that the crashed plane belonged to Eastern Airlines, which became a source of one piece of misinformation that propagated in early news coverage of the event.

The calls kept coming, forcing the emergency communications center to sort out conflicting information. Some callers said it was a small plane, others said it was a 737. It was unclear whether the plane had passengers, whether it was on the bridge or in the water.

Nobody in the dispatch center had experience handling an incident of this scale. Nothing like this had ever happened. And it was happening at the worst time, during a crippling blizzard.

Souder set the fast-food bag down on the dispatch desk and reclaimed his seat at the microphone. This was the time for a trusted voice.

The Vocalarm loudspeaker in Engine Company 16's equipment room echoed with a series of tones, followed by the sound of Souder's voice: "Box 1, Engine 2, 13, 16, and 7; fireboat, Box 10 and 3, chief 6, rescue squads 1, 2, 3, and foam wagon. Respond to report of an Eastern Airlines plane down off the 14th Street Bridge on Box 417."

The orders dispatched three fire trucks, two engines, three of the city's four rescue squads, and five ambulances, directing them to the location of the closest fire box. The initial response included a specialized crash unit and a truck equipped with lights. A crew was dispatched to power up the city's fireboat, the *John H. Glenn Jr.*, docked at the southwest waterfront.

Fire department vehicles encountered nearly overwhelming obstacles that slowed their response to the Potomac. They needed to get to the farthest point of the District of Columbia, at the boundary with Virginia, on snowbound streets gridlocked with rush-hour traffic.

As the firehouse doors swung open, Engine 16 faced a wall of vehicles on 13th Street. Leaning on the siren was of no use; there was nowhere for cars to move out of the way. Dean ordered his firefighters to walk in front of the truck, directing cars and moving them if necessary, to clear a path.

The men of Engine 16 went from vehicle to vehicle, slowly advancing a block at a time. Traveling three miles from the fire station to the 14th Street Bridge took thirteen minutes.

The District of Columbia's emergency operations center activated the five-state Washington Area Emergency Civil Defense Communications network, alerting hundreds of fire departments in Maryland, Virginia, Delaware, West Virginia, and North Carolina, as well as police agencies in Maryland and Virginia, the Federal Bureau of Investigation, and the Department of Transportation.

4:08 P.M.

National Airport's deputy fire chief implemented the airport's disaster plan and broadcast an urgent message on the civil defense radio network: "National Airport to all emergency services involved in emergency planning for the airport. We have a report of a 737 down by the 14th Street Bridge."

National used the radio network to request the District of Columbia Fire Department, the fireboat, and the harbor police boat. They alerted the Red Cross, Bolling Air Force Base, St. Elizabeths Hospital, and Fort Belvoir, a large army base in Fairfax County, Virginia, for assistance. Fort Belvoir dispatched four Bell UH-1 Huey military helicopters toward Washington. But they would take awhile.

Primary responsibility for rescues on navigable waterways lies with the Coast Guard. But the Coast Guard's sixty-five-foot ice-breaking tug *Capstan* was engaged on a search-and-rescue mission down the river in Mount Vernon. Traveling through the ice at half speed, it would take three hours for *Capstan* to respond to the 14th Street Bridge.

Not even a snowstorm could spoil Ruby Mae Thomas's radiant mood. She had just finished an interview and landed a dream job at a computer firm on Wilson Avenue in Fairfax, an ideal match for her background in programming and administration.

The thirty-year-old Thomas dressed the part of a professional woman on the move: knee-high leather boots, long leather jacket, and a brown leather briefcase to complete the ensemble. She looked sharp and felt sharp. Now all she had to do was pick up her two young children from her mother's apartment in New Carrollton, where they'd gone after school.

Thomas descended into the Rosslyn station of the Metro Blue/Orange Line. The platform was crowded with people leaving work early. She boarded the first car of train 410 and took a seat toward the back.

At the next station, Foggy Bottom–GWU, Thomas stood to give her seat to an elderly gentleman as more passengers boarded.

A native of Yonkers, John Brazier was a volunteer emergency medical technician (EMT) at a time when the field was new and *Emergency!*, with Roy DeSoto and John Gage, still aired on television. He took pride in being part of the revolution in prehospital medical care, saving lives when minutes mattered. He'd thought he made the major league when he was hired by the New York City Fire Department, until the city fell on hard times in the 1970s and cut back on public services.

The District of Columbia Fire Department was recruiting, so Brazier answered the call. When he arrived in the city, he asked for the busiest ambulance in the department. "I come from Yonkers," he told the recruiter. "I want busy."

The department put Brazier on Medic 5, ranked the busiest ambulance in the nation according to an annual survey conducted by *Firehouse* magazine. Medic 5 is based at Engine Company 6 station at 1100 New Jersey Avenue NW, which itself was ranked in *Firehouse* magazine as the busiest fire station in the United States five years in a row.

The call volume at Engine Company 6 was so grueling that assignment to the station was sometimes meted out as punishment. But Brazier relished the action.

Brazier had just dropped off a patient at George Washington University Hospital when Souder barked through the two-way radio, "Respond to report of an Eastern Airlines plane down off the 14th Street Bridge on Box 417."

Medic 5 was not included in the initial response. By this time, Brazier was done with work for the day. He and his partner could return to the station and be relieved by the next shift. Brazier keyed his mic and asked if they should also respond to the call.

Yes, Souder said.

Whoa, this must be something serious, Brazier thought. *To send an ambulance from the middle of DC to the 14th Street Bridge, it's gotta be something big.*

Desperately clinging to a jagged shred of fuselage, Duncan grew increasingly agitated at the growing crowd on the bridge and gathering along the Potomac, gawking but not doing anything to help. She was angry.

"We're going to die out here," she screamed.

A motorist on the HOV bridge threw a rope over the railing, dangling about forty feet away from the tail section. "Take the rope," he yelled.

Joe Stiley weighed his options. He'd have to let go of the fuselage and make it thirty to forty feet through open water. And then what? Even if he could reach the rope, he couldn't raise himself out of the water with one good arm. He could be going from a bad situation to something worse. And he couldn't abandon Nikki Felch, his assistant. Even at the risk of hypothermia, it made sense to stay together on the wreckage.

"Fire trucks are on the way," somebody yelled from the bridge.

"We don't need a fire truck," Bert Hamilton yelled back. "We need a boat."

Less than 10 percent of commercial aviation incidents occur midflight. Ninety percent of crashes are related to takeoff or landing and happen within ten miles of the airport.

Many US cities have major commercial airports near significant bodies of water, including Baltimore, Boston, Chicago, Houston, Jacksonville, Los Angeles, Miami, New Orleans, New York, Philadelphia, San Francisco, San Diego, and Seattle. Tens of millions of passengers fly out of these airports annually.

During the two decades preceding the crash of Flight 90, what aviation parlance euphemistically calls an "unplanned water entry" of a commercial airliner had occurred at least once every year.

On March 10, 1979, Swift Aire Flight 235, a Nord 262 propeller-driven aircraft on scheduled service to Santa Monica, California, departed from Los Angeles International Airport with four passengers and three crew members. The plane experienced engine failure on takeoff and ditched at Marina del Rey, sinking in twelve feet of water. Two pilots and one passenger drowned.

On the foggy night of May 8, 1978, National Airlines Flight 193, a Boeing 727 with fifty-two passengers and a crew of five, was approaching Pensacola Regional Airport in low visibility when the pilot lost situational awareness and crashed into Escambia Bay. Three passengers drowned, and eleven people were injured.

On September 14, 1972, the pilot of a TWA Boeing 707 aborted a takeoff from San Francisco International Airport. The plane overran the runway and splashed into the San Francisco Bay. The three crew members aboard, the only occupants of the plane, were unharmed.

Despite the clear risks to the traveling public, FAA regulations didn't require airports located near bodies of water to have water rescue capabilities.

Although not required by regulation, National Airport had a single water rescue craft. It was an airboat, with a flat bottom and a large fan mounted on the deck for propulsion. Airboats are commonly used to cruise through the Everglades swamps.

In many respects, using an airboat as a rescue craft makes sense. They move quickly through the water, don't have a propeller that could pose a risk to victims in the water, and are advantageous in areas of the Potomac that are shallow. The plan in the event of a water intrusion near National Airport was to respond quickly and distribute flotation devices to victims.

Airboats are less useful on ice, particularly during a storm.

They're more difficult to maneuver on ice and tend to get pushed around by crosswinds. And whether on water or ice, airboats are difficult to steer at low speeds.

Airport firefighters tried rolling the trailer carrying the airboat down the snow-covered concrete boat ramp to no avail. So the firefighters picked up the boat and carried it into the water.

The boat ramp at National is at the southern end of the airport. Once the airboat was placed on the frozen surface, firefighters had to navigate around the length of the airport and across more than two miles of solid ice.

National Airport's fire department conducted a training exercise in July 1978 involving an airliner ditching into the Potomac River, with mannequins in the water substituting for survivors. The drill was observed by members of the Air Line Pilots Association (ALPA), who described an almost comically disorganized scene. Equipment used by first responders was minimal and ineffective. Pilots criticized the airboat as underpowered and poorly equipped, with limited seaworthiness that made it inappropriate as a primary rescue craft.

First responders used pointed pike poles to pluck mannequins out of the water and stacked them up on the rescue craft to the extent that, had they been the weight of real human remains, they would have dangerously overloaded the boat.

The performance of first responders improved with subsequent exercises. The Prince George's County Fire Department conducted a large-scale disaster exercise in the summer of 1979 based on an airplane crash that included simulated victims and the involvement of other governmental agencies.

National Airport's most recent mock disaster had been held in the summer of 1981. Members of the Prince George's County Fire Department were allowed to observe the exercise, but no other agencies were directly involved.

For each of the training exercises, participants knew the time, location, and nature of the incident in advance. In real life, first responders can't choose the timing and circumstances for catastrophe to strike.

All the mock disaster drills were conducted during warm weather. Ice was a factor that had never been contemplated.

In December 1980, ALPA had submitted a petition to the FAA describing the deplorable state of preparations for water rescue at domestic airports, specifically citing Washington National as a facility vulnerable to water incidents. The pilots' union made several recommendations to improve life rafts, flotation devices, and water rescue preparations.

One year later, a month before the crash of Flight 90, the FAA circulated proposed changes to technical service orders (TSOs), which incorporated many of ALPA's suggestions. No further action had been taken.

Firefighters aboard the fireboat *John H. Glenn Jr.* reported that the boat was icebound at the dock. Ice four inches thick blocked the air intake for the engine and needed to be chipped away. The fire department requested the assistance of a commercial sand and gravel tug, *Papa John*, to help break the ice around the fireboat.

Metro Police had several inflatable Zodiac-type boats and a patrol boat with a fiberglass hull, none of which were suitable for ice conditions. A fiberglass hull is no match against thick ice. Moving through ice of any substantial thickness requires a steel hull. Neither the Metro Police nor the harbor patrol had steel-hulled boats.

The District of Columbia activated its emergency operations center and issued an urgent request for any available watercraft in the area. The harbor patrol commandeered an excursion boat docked at the southwest waterfront; it joined a slow-moving armada that included three police boats and a privately owned yacht.

Once the fireboat could be started and freed from its docking, once the nautical resources could be rallied, they would still have to travel through the ice nearly a mile and a half around Hains Point at the tip of East Potomac Park to the crash scene.

Roger Olian's progress through the water was agonizingly slow. His hands and feet were deadened by the cold, making his efforts more laborious. Bystanders on the bank of the Potomac lengthened the lifeline around his waist, adding more jumper cables and extension cords and feeding it out to the water.

Olian yanked on the awkward restraint and inched farther, spitting out foul-tasting water tainted with jet fuel. Every breath was odious.

He felt a tug back to shore. "What the hell," he muttered. A bystander shouted that a rescue boat was on the way.

Olian scanned the bleak expanse of ice. "That's crazy," he yelled back.

"Okay, keep going for the plane," said the voice from shore.

"I'm trying to," Olian said.

Displaced possessions littered the Potomac around the avulsed airframe. The contents of overhead bins were scattered amid the slush and ice. Clothing. Shoes. A tennis racket zipped in its bag.

Nikki Felch found a flotation vest, a bright-yellow brick-like package hermetically sealed in a durable clear plastic pouch. She pawed at the package but couldn't tear it open with frozen, injured hands. She bit into the plastic and chewed open a small hole. She handed the package to Kelly Duncan, and the flight attendant tore at the hole with her teeth. Together the women ripped the pouch far enough open to extract the folded vest.

Felch offered the vest to Duncan, thinking that it might help ease her agitated state. Duncan handed it back. Even with a fractured arm, Felch managed to get the vest over her head and buckled around her ribs.

Joe Stiley saw another flotation vest package near Arland Williams and asked him to pass it over.

"I can't reach it," Williams told him. "I can't move my arms."

The flotation vest used by commercial airlines, known as the Mark 1, was developed during World War II. The basic design of the Mark 1 has remained unchanged ever since.

It's secured by two straps around the chest; two bladders in the front can be inflated by a self-contained CO_2 cartridge. Because of the buxom appearance of the wearer when inflated, the Mark I was nicknamed the Mae West after the Hollywood actress.

The Mark I is not an ideal flotation vest for commercial aviation. It was designed for the military, not civilians, and was meant to be put on before a flight and worn for the duration. On commercial airliners, the vests were folded up and stored beneath the seats, which tended to collapse during a water impact. In the darkness and confusion after a water crash, it could be difficult to retrieve the vest with another passenger's belongings under the seat, then put the vest on, and secure the two straps correctly. Most of the inflatable components of the Mark I are on the front of the body, which tends to put the wearer on their back in water. An inexperienced swimmer may have difficulty keeping their head out of the water.

4:09 P.M.

Inside the trailer used by the park police aviation unit, the telephone rang. Rescue technician Ron Galey answered the call. It was the tower at National Airport.

"Are you guys flying?" an air traffic manager asked.

Don Usher and the other park police pilots had a friendly collegial relationship with the National Airport tower. Among the few pilots allowed in the tightly controlled

A truck hit by Flight 90 dangles from the damaged 14th Street Bridge. Associated Press

airspace over the District of Columbia, Usher would occasionally land Eagle One beside the tower and take air traffic controllers for a ride to show them what pilots see during approach and departure. It is an invaluable experience that gives them a greater appreciation for the unique challenges of flying in and out of the airport.

"No. What's going on?" Galey asked.

"We aren't sure, but we may have a plane missing," the manager said. The plane could have gone into Roaches Run, a body of water between the end of Runway 36 and the Twin Bridges Marriott, or somewhere farther up the Potomac.

Weather conditions were atrocious. Visibility was down to a quarter mile, with a ceiling of two hundred feet and heavy snowfall. Flying in these conditions without instruments is extremely risky, outside of operational guidelines. But the area is bordered by Potomac Park on one side and the George Washington Memorial Parkway on the other, both of which are park police jurisdiction.

As the park police's chief pilot, the final decision was up to Usher.

"Let's go," he said.

The tarmac runway in front of the park police hangar was covered with several inches of snow. Galey had a side job plowing driveways and parking lots and had driven to work with the plow blade on the front of his truck. He plowed the area in front of the hangar while Usher and Windsor, usually assigned to Eagle Two, prepared Eagle One for flight.

The Bell helicopters used by the park police are utility craft, designed for surveillance and routine law enforcement support. They are among the lightest possible aircraft able to patrol over urban areas. Eagle One and Eagle Two can carry a gurney for medevac flights but are not intended for rescue missions.

The helicopters are not equipped with rescue equipment — no basket to hold victims, no hoist to lift up to the helicopter, no ropes or rescue nets. Windsor looked around the hangar for anything that might be helpful and found a rescue buoy — a yellow plastic ball that self-inflates when it hits water and deploys a personal flotation device.

With skids rather than wheels, the park police helicopters can't be pushed on their own. When not in use, the helicopters are on trailers. Usher and Windsor pushed Eagle One's trailer onto the tarmac. Usher ran through the preflight checklist at breakneck speed and powered up the helicopter while Galey returned his truck alongside the hangar. Windsor hopped into Eagle One and buckled up.

Usher keyed the radio and notified National's tower that they were going to take off.

"Eagle One, do not depart," the air traffic controller replied. "The field is experiencing an emergency."

"I'm aware of that," Usher said. "We're responding to the emergency."

"Okay, go ahead."

Within four minutes of receiving the phone call from National Airport, Eagle One departed the Eagle's Nest, rising into the air and turning to the northwest across the Anacostia River.

Corporal Thomas Hoffman of the Arlington County Police was finishing up in the emergency department of the National Hospital for Orthopaedics and Rehabilitation, known by locals as just National Hospital.

Its stately name notwithstanding, National Hospital was a small privately owned community hospital. Founded in the 1940s as a clinic for children with poliomyelitis, over the years the hospital grew into a 129-bed facility specializing in the treatment of bone and joint disorders.

National Hospital didn't have an intensive care unit or offer specialty medical care like cardiology or labor and delivery. Its modest three-room emergency department lacked the sophisticated resources of a Level 1 trauma center, such as MedStar Washington Hospital Center or the university-affiliated hospitals in Washington. At times, there wasn't even a board-certified emergency physician on duty. Still, National Hospital's emergency department was adequate for setting broken bones and suturing lacerations.

As the first-line police supervisor on duty, Hoffman had been busy since his shift began at 3:00 P.M. He was at National Hospital's emergency department to get information for an accident report when his police radio squawked: A small plane may have gone down at National Airport. It could be in Roaches Run.

Hoffman found traffic on I-395 headed north toward Washington at a standstill. He decided against taking the ramp onto I-395 and remained on city streets. With chains on his squad car tires, Hoffman made steady progress on roads that were relatively clear of other vehicles. He rolled down Army Navy Drive, which runs parallel to the interstate past the Pentagon, to Boundary Channel Drive.

Using the shoulder to go around stalled traffic, Hoffman took the off-ramp and headed south on the George Washington Memorial Parkway. Ahead of him, approaching from the direction of National Airport, he saw the flashing lights of emergency vehicles. The driver of the lead fire truck waved Hoffman over, so he drove across the median and followed the vehicles to the 14th Street Bridge.

Parking on the bridge, Hoffman stood and surveyed the eerily quiet yet staggering scene of destruction. He looked inside a brown Audi sedan with its roof sheared off. The driver, an air force officer on his way home from the Pentagon, was decapitated. In front of the Audi was a crane truck tipped on its side. Several other cars were damaged, and an unknown number of people trapped and injured. A chunk of the concrete bridge wall was missing.

Pieces of a commercial airliner floated in the Potomac. The skin of the fuselage had peeled away like a banana skin, leaving passengers visible beneath the surface of the water still strapped in their seats.

Hoffman's radio report to police headquarters was the first indication of the scale of the disaster.

"There are bodies everywhere," he told the dispatcher.

Without any rescue equipment in his squad car, Hoffman could do little more but step back and let trained first responders do their work.

The Eastern Airlines plane bringing Arlington County detectives Tom Panther and Butch Gressley back from Florida crossed paths with Flight 90 on the National Airport runway. The cops had in their custody a nineteen-year-old habitual car thief whose flirtation with freedom had ended in Tallahassee. Once they disembarked, Panther called police headquarters to have a squad car pick them up at the airport.

"Nobody is available," Panther told Gressley. "They said to take a cab."

"I think I heard over a policeman's radio that they had a crash here," Gressley said.

"I didn't hear anything," Panther replied.

The men and their detainee hailed a cab that took them north on the George Washington Memorial Parkway. Nearing the 14th Street Bridge, they saw two emergency vehicles, their lights flashing, pull off the side of the road. Neither police officer knew the significance of what they witnessed.

4:11 P.M.

John Harris drove National Airport's ambulance over the curb of George Washington Memorial Parkway and parked near the edge of the bluff leading down to the Potomac riverbank. Red 396, one of the airport's firefighting/crash trucks, pulled up alongside the ambulance. A knot of bystanders, including many in military uniforms, had gathered by the water.

The crash truck carried foam and firefighting equipment, but no rescue gear. Neither emergency vehicle was equipped with rope or a flotation device or anything that could rescue victims from the water. First responders could do nothing but watch Roger Olian wade farther out into the ice.

Since departing from National Airport for their work assignment, Chester Panzer and George Patterson had made little progress on the George Washington Memorial Parkway. Traffic was a sluggish crawl. It was going to take

Vehicles on the 14th Street Bridge struck by Flight 90. Ira Schwarz / Associated Press

a long while for Panzer to drive Patterson to his home in Arlington. They were listening to music when the WJLA news desk squawked over the two-way radio.

"What's your location?" the assignment editor asked.

"We're on the GW Parkway south of Arlington Memorial Bridge," Patterson responded.

The men listened as the station queried other field reporters. Nobody else was in the vicinity.

"We heard that a plane may have crashed at National Airport," the assignment editor said. "Go check it out."

National Airport was about two miles in the opposite direction, behind them. Panzer pulled the crew car to the left and drove through deep snow across the wide median to the southbound side of George Washington Memorial

Parkway, which had very little traffic. Patterson tuned the radio to WTOP.

Mary L. O'Meara and Mildred M. Morgan were coworkers at the Overseas Education Association (OEA), an organization representing faculty and staff in the Department of Defense school system. The OEA was a very small organization, with only five full-time employees.

O'Meara, twenty-five, had graduated from law school the year before and worked for the OEA as deputy legal counsel. She planned to get married in July. Morgan, seventy-one, was semi-retired and worked as a secretary three days a week.

The women didn't usually commute together. But when the office closed early, they decided to keep each other company trudging through the snow to the McPherson Square Metro station.

O'Meara was taking the Blue/Orange train to the end of the line at New Carrollton, where her father would be waiting as usual to pick her up. Morgan was going eight stops on the same line to the Potomac Avenue station, then taking a WMATA bus a short distance to a restaurant where she'd meet her husband, William Morgan, for dinner.

Stepping aboard train 410, Morgan sat next to Mariano Cortez, a forty-six-year-old auditor for the Department of Agriculture, on inward-facing seats near the middle side door. Instead of trying to fight traffic all the way home, Cortez had left his Plymouth at work and opted for the Metro. O'Meara found a seat near where Ruby Mae

Thomas stood, holding her leather briefcase tight in the increasingly crowded train car.

The next stop was Metro Center.

John Brazier drove Medic 5 down Virginia Avenue at a snail's pace. At Constitution Avenue, the northern edge of the National Mall, he faced a mass of traffic converging on the bridges to Northern Virginia.

He needed to make a left turn on Constitution Avenue, to the east toward 14th Street. Vehicles had no room to pull over for him, but the sidewalk was wide enough for the ambulance, so he drove over the curb and slowly rolled down the sidewalk across the Ellipse in front of the White House.

Lurching through the ice-bogged water, Roger Olian began to question the wisdom of his hasty actions. The improvised jumper cable tether around his waist kept snagging on ice, hindering his progress. He was still fully clothed, wearing steel-toed boots and a jacket. The massive ring of work keys in his pocket felt like five pounds tugging him down.

It was exhausting. Olian paused to catch his breath. His hands and feet felt like insensible clubs, so cold he couldn't flex his fingers. He went into the water thinking that he could save the people clinging to the fragment of fuselage in the middle of the river. Now he wondered what he could do if he made it to them. He couldn't save them all. Maybe he could save one person. Saving one life would be worthwhile.

"Hang on," Olian yelled to huddled survivors. "Help is on the way."

4:14 P.M.

A helicopter consists of thousands of moving parts constantly trying to rip it apart. Flying a helicopter is very different from piloting a fixed-wing aircraft. Airplanes are stable by nature. Let go of the controls, and an airplane will continue level flight, at least for a while. If something goes wrong during flight, the crew usually has the luxury of minutes to figure out a solution.

Helicopters are inherently unstable mechanical beasts. Without a pilot's continuous engagement with both hands and both feet, a helicopter will quickly whip chaotically out of control. In the left hand, the twist-grip collective regulates the engine power and movement up and down. The cyclic stick in the right hand governs the direction the helicopter is traveling. Foot pedals guide turning along the yaw axis, to the left and right. Maneuvering a helicopter through three-dimensional space is a carefully controlled pas de deux between human and machine.

Don Usher lifted off in whiteout conditions. His entire field of view was obliterated by a swirling white mass of snow. As with the wings of an airplane, ice can form on the rotors of a helicopter and interfere with lift. But helicopters don't have anti-icing systems like a commercial airliner. Snow and ice were problems as soon as Eagle One lifted off the tarmac, splattering and sticking to the windshield.

Although National Airport was directly to the west, flying across the Potomac was too risky. Lacking the ground-sensing equipment of an airplane, Usher could become disoriented and crash into the water. His only option was to fly over the city.

The massive snowstorm pushed the clouds down to two hundred feet above the ground, nearly to the height of Washington's office buildings. Usher had to fly low to remain under the ceiling, in the turbulent air layer just beneath the clouds. Helicopter pilots call it scud-running, a choppy, bone-rattling ride.

Usher knew that air traffic in the area was shut down. The sky was all his for now, with no concern about striking another aircraft. And there were no power lines to worry about; all utilities in the area are buried. Because of height restrictions — by law no structure in the District of Columbia can be taller than the US Capitol — Usher also knew he didn't have to worry about any radio towers or high-rise buildings in their way. That left a very narrow path for Eagle One.

"Don, how can you fly in this?" Windsor asked.

"Following traffic," Usher said.

Flying just above the level of the streetlights, Usher traced a route he knew well, Anacostia Drive to South Capitol Street, then following the string of taillights over the bridge across the Anacostia River. The misfortune of commuters was a godsend for Eagle One, as a trail of red lights blazed a path through the storm.

A swarm of emergency vehicles slowly snaked through the streets of Arlington. Howard Piansky was behind the wheel of Engine 75, a Simon-Duplex Saulsbury pumper that had just returned to service from the maintenance shop that morning. Trained as an EMT/paramedic like many of the county's firefighters, Piansky was detailed as a driver at Station 5, the closest to the 14th Street Bridge.

Richmond Highway, the main route through Crystal City, was hopelessly snarled. Piansky thought it would be quicker to cut over to George Washington Memorial Parkway, but Captain McClintock, in the passenger seat next to him, insisted that he take I-395, straight through the thick of traffic. The captain's the boss, so that's the direction Piansky drove.

Leaving the expressway, Piansky ran over a curb concealed beneath a snowdrift and managed to tear up the clutch. With the wagon incapacitated, McClintock ordered the men to walk the remaining quarter mile to the 14th Street Bridge. Had Piansky taken the route he suggested, they would have pulled up on the parkway right at the scene.

In terms of medical schools and hospitals, Washington boasts an embarrassment of riches. Three medical schools — at Howard, Georgetown, and George Washington Universities — have highly regarded teaching hospitals in the city. Also nearby are Bethesda Naval Hospital, Walter Reed Medical Center, the National Institutes of Health campus, and the Uniformed Services University of the Health Sciences medical school.

George Washington University's MedStar Medical Center stands out. Its trauma center is accredited as Level 1, capable of treating the most critically injured patients. When an assassination attempt had been made on President Reagan nine months earlier, he was taken to the MedStar emergency department.

According to the District of Columbia's disaster plan, hospitals must be notified when a multiple-casualty incident happens. The fire department communications office is supposed to contact hospitals to learn their capacity, give them advance notice that patients may be incoming, and let them know when the crisis is over.

The District of Columbia Hospital Association devised a disaster plan in which one hospital in Washington would be designated as a clearinghouse for information on patient care capabilities from all the hospitals and relay that information to the incident scene so that patients could be distributed to hospitals on some rational basis.

None of these thoroughly considered plans were implemented. Instead, hospitals had to rely on word-of-mouth or radio and television news coverage of the disasters, and patients were taken to whatever hospital the ambulance drivers chose.

Dr. William Fouty, chief of surgery at MedStar Washington Hospital Center, heard about the plane crash on WTOP radio. Fouty called Robert Hartley, a park police pilot he knew through their work together at the trauma center, to find out what was happening. Then he announced a code 777 — the hospital's highest emergency alert.

Within minutes, thirty-nine doctors gathered around six critical care beds in the trauma unit by the helipad. They were organized into ten surgical teams. Twenty-nine additional doctors stood ready in the emergency room next door. With personnel and sophisticated equipment at the ready, they waited for the arrival of victims.

But the call never came.

On the other side of the Potomac, Dr. Richard Schwartz, chief of medicine at National Hospital, was driving his BMW through Rosslyn on his way home. He was stuck in a traffic jam when he heard an unconfirmed report of a plane crash on the radio.

Schwartz got out of his car and walked to the tractor-trailer in front of him. "I'm a doctor," he told the driver, "and I have a problem."

Apprised of the urgency, the trucker pulled out and blocked traffic so Schwartz could do a U-turn and head back to the hospital. He used his portable telephone to call ahead and order the hospital to a Code Yellow alert, the facility's highest state of readiness. The lobby was cleared for the arrival of victims, with more than thirty doctors standing by.

Looking down through the nose bubble between his feet, Usher steered Eagle One toward the South Capitol Street bridge and northward to the right.

The white-and-blue park police helicopter was a striking sight, flying just above the streetlights between the buildings up South Capitol Street. Along the way Usher was receiving conflicting radio transmission updates from the tower; the downed plane could be as far as Theodore Roosevelt Island, or in Potomac Park. He repeatedly tried to get through on the Police Mutual Aid Radio System, the frequency shared by nineteen agencies in the Washington area, but nobody responded to him.

At no time did any official activate PMARS and designate the mutual aid channel as the official command frequency, which was its intended purpose. Even if PMARS had been employed, hand-held radios couldn't use the system. Each agency could only communicate with its own personnel.

The line of vehicle lights on South Capitol Street led to the tangle of ramps and bridges at the interchange with I-395. With their limited visibility, Usher and Windsor could see that traffic on the outbound span of the 14th Street Bridge into Virginia was bumper-to-bumper. But the inbound span of the bridge was dark, with no traffic at all. Usher nosed the helicopter to the left, over the bridge, heading toward Virginia.

Roger Olian dragged himself across the field of broken ice until he reached the edge of the hole the plane had punched through the ice. A few yards of open water remained between him and the victims; he was close enough to see their faces.

Olian didn't know what to do. He was fatigued and hypothermic. His arms and legs were practically useless. It felt as if he were moving though syrup. Going any farther would mean unfastening the tether and swimming out to the fuselage. And then what? He didn't know if he had the strength to swim to the wreckage and back. At this point, he wasn't sure he would make it out of the water alive. Maybe it would be enough to provide moral support. Maybe his reckless gesture would at least show them that somebody was trying to do something to help.

"You can't give up," Olian yelled to the survivors. "You gotta hold on."

The fuselage was unstable and slippery, a hulking structure slowly rotating and sinking in the water. Holding on to its smooth surface with senseless nubs for hands was becoming impossible.

"Are you okay?" Joe Stiley asked Arland Williams, separated by a shred of the fuselage.

"I'm not going to make it," Williams said.

"Yeah you will," Stiley said. "Somebody will be here. Don't worry about it. We'll be all right."

"We'll never get out," Williams said. "We're all going to die."

Stiley tried to be encouraging, but realistically their prospects were grim. Snow caked on his eyebrows. The survivors had been in freezing water for twenty minutes and were no closer to being rescued. They wouldn't last much longer. As the minutes ticked by, it became increasingly obvious that their situation was hopeless.

The others were resigned to their fate. Bert Hamilton led the group in the Lord's Prayer: *Our Father, who art in heaven, hallowed be thy name . . .*

Through the clouds in the distance emerged a deep, guttural sound: *whoomp whoomp whoomp whoomp . . .*

4:21 P.M.

The Metro Center station is the hub of the Metrorail system. The transfer point between the Blue/Orange and the Red Lines, it is the largest and busiest of the Metro stations.

On an afternoon of endless delays, train 410 was the first northbound Blue/Orange train to New Carrollton to stop at Metro Center in thirty-four minutes. The platform was thronged with commuters who had been waiting to get home. When the doors opened, riders piled into the train's six cars.

Each of Metrorail's cars was designed to comfortably accommodate a maximum of around 180 commuters, with seats for 80 and the rest standing. When train 410 left the Metro Center station, 200 to 220 riders were in each of the six cars. The train reached what the WMATA terms crush capacity, with thirteen hundred or more passengers packed shoulder-to-shoulder.

The next station would be Federal Triangle.

As though on cue, the torrent of snow eased up. For the first time all day, precipitation diminished to a light sprinkle of flakes.

Skimming over the deserted span of the 14th Street Bridge, Usher and Windsor observed some damaged vehicles and flashing emergency lights near the Virginia side. It looked like a traffic accident.

As Eagle One approached Virginia, the officers found an inexplicable scene. This was a plane crash? There was no smoke, no scorch marks, no debris field, nothing but a black hole in an expanse of white ice with cracks radiating outward. Like a baseball had been thrown through a pane of glass. Where was the plane?

Initially, Usher and Windsor thought perhaps a small plane had gone into the water, until they got closer and discerned the tail section of an airliner jutting out with Air Florida's distinctive blue-and-green logo.

The officers tried to make sense of what they were seeing. Usher figured that if a 737 had gone down, those dozens of people gathered along the bank of the Potomac must have been passengers who somehow made it to shore. The ones in the water must have been the unfortunates who didn't make it out.

Usher circled to the right, hovering over the water to blow away debris and allow Windsor to better visualize the victims.

The surface of the water was littered with clothing, uphol-stery, the assorted contents of luggage, aircraft insulation, and personal belongings blown around by the helicopter's powerful prop wash. If a single piece of debris were kicked up and struck a rotor, that could bring the helicopter down and kill them all. Usher considered how to undertake a rescue and remain alive.

Olian gestured to the park police helicopter. "Okay, you guys can take it from here," he said.

"I count seven in the water," Windsor told Usher. "Some are hurt pretty bad."

Most of the victims were grouped together, holding on to a piece of fuselage. Three of them were visibly bleeding from the head. Usher pointed out one person by himself by the edge of the ice hole, near open water. Deciding that this man was most at risk, he directed Eagle One toward Olian first.

"No, not me," Olian yelled at the helicopter, pointing to the crash survivors. "Them, over there!"

The bystanders on land pulled the improvised tether to reel in Olian. He watched Eagle One deftly maneuver as he bobbed through the water. *That's a hotshot Vietnam pilot,* he thought to himself. He had seen those guys do unreal things with helicopters in the war. *He knows what he's doing.*

Usher watched Olian drift backward toward shore. "He's okay," he said to Windsor, turning Eagle One toward the wreckage in the water.

Olian was unable to stand when he reached the shore. His legs felt like stumps. De La Cruz helped drag Olian from the water. Ice clung to Olian's clothing and filled the pockets of his jacket. His limp, waterlogged body was carried to a nearby Jeep, where the heat was turned up high. Olian sat in the front passenger seat and began to shiver violently.

4:22 P.M.

ABC News anchor Frank Reynolds interrupted the afternoon soap opera *The Edge of Night* with a breaking news bulletin. The information was preliminary and incomplete, as the incident was still ongoing.

"There has been a dreadful airplane crash in Washington," Reynolds said to the camera. "An Air Florida 737, a short while ago, after taking off from National Airport bound for Tampa, struck a bridge, the 14th Street Bridge in Washington . . . We understand that the plane, a 737 jet capable of carrying about eighty people, struck the bridge, hit about four cars and a truck, and careened on into the river. We have one report that there are some survivors in the water. Some people have been picked up and taken to George Washington University Hospital, which you'll recall was where President Reagan was taken after the assassination attempt against him. That is basically all we know at this point. It is probably weather-related because Washington is experiencing a very, very bad snowstorm here today, part of the tremendous storm that has afflicted so much of the country. Another factor to be kept in mind is that the government, because of the storm, is in effect closed down, and the bridges going across to Virginia have been heavily jammed with homeward-bound commuters . . ."

Over the next hours, Reynolds interrupted regular programming with updated reports as information developed.

Once the morning peak period passed, Metrorail's trains were back on schedule. Problems cropped up again midafternoon, compounded by the early release of federal employees.

A train stalled at the Foggy Bottom–GWU station, causing extended delays. Another train out of New Carrollton experienced repeated braking problems. A Red Line train had propulsion problems. Three trains broke down during a twenty-minute period. Since the early rush hour began, four trains had been taken out of service, and thirty-four others had been canceled.

Problems were occurring so quickly that it was difficult for OCC personnel to concentrate on any one of them. In terms of Metro breakdowns and delays, this was the worst day that assistant superintendent Paul Hobgood Jr. had seen in his seven years on the job.

Blue/Orange train 403, bound for National Airport, stopped at the Federal Triangle Metro station platform at around 3:45. The train operator heard an explosion beneath the train, which suddenly lost power. Passengers were offloaded at the Federal Triangle station, already congested because of the early rush hour.

Although train 403 wouldn't go forward, the operator was able to move it in reverse. The OCC decided to have the operator back the train to the maintenance yard at New Carrollton. To do that safely, train 403 would have to shift over to the northbound D-1 track.

Metrorail trains change tracks in a section of tunnel called an interlocking, where the two tubes merge together and the rails form an X. Interlockings are used to reverse the direction of a train, or to temporarily move a train out of the way to let another pass.

As the Metrorail system was originally designed, the

crossovers were not intended to be used frequently. The interlockings were meant to preserve continuous use of the Metrorail system during emergencies or unusual situations. In practice, the WMATA operations had evolved to routinely use the crossovers, nearly on a daily basis.

One of these crossovers — the Smithsonian Interlocking — is sixty feet beneath the National Mall, between the Smithsonian's Museum of American History and the Museum of Natural History.

At the Smithsonian Interlocking, one of the four switches had been causing problems for days, tripping a fuse that necessitated setting the switch by hand. Switch 1-A, at one end of one of the rails, occasionally wouldn't return to its original position for normal travel. The problem had been noted on January 10, three days earlier, but hadn't been considered a critical issue because rail supervisors in the tunnels could inspect the switches to make sure they were properly set.

Until the switch could be repaired, tracks at the interlocking would have a red light, meaning that operators would have to take trains out of automatic mode and proceed by driving trains manually through the crossover.

Before sending train 403 out of service to New Carrollton, the OCC had it wait in the Smithsonian Interlocking so six trains headed to National Airport that had been waiting could go around it.

Once the six trains were detoured, the OCC asked rail supervisor James Davis to manually set the four switches because one of them was balking. the OCC told Davis to set the switch to align the tracks — tuck them under, in their jargon — and lock them in place with yellow wood blocks. The foot-long wood blocks, with WMATA stenciled on them in black lettering, were a backup mechanism to ensure that switches stayed in position. Four blocks would be used, one for each switch.

Train 403 was switched over to the northbound D-1 track through the Smithsonian Interlocking without problem and continued to the end of the line at the New Carrollton rail yard.

The OCC directed Davis to set the switches back to normal travel. "Supervisor Davis, is track 1 blocked now?" controller Kenneth Banks asked over the radio.

"Roger," Davis replied. "All switches are blocked and tucked under at this time."

"All right," Banks said. "Stay there and wave the trains through, would you please?"

"Roger, my pleasure," Davis replied.

4:23 P.M.

James Schneider had been contending with the snow all day. A maintenance manager at Arlington Hospital, Schneider's priority was keeping the 350-bed acute care facility functioning. He had men working snowplows to clear driveways and parking lots, and a crew of thirty-five with shovels to keep sidewalks free of snow.

At shift change time, Schneider's men used four-wheel-drive vehicles to shuttle doctors and nurses unable to get in on their own. The hospital's essential services couldn't be paused for a blizzard.

Schneider was sitting in the office of his boss, James Felch, the hospital's director of engineering and maintenance. Felch was a retired colonel who had spent a career with the Army Corps of Engineers.

The phone rang and Felch picked it up. It was David Frank, who had just gotten engaged to Felch's daughter, Nikki. Frank worked at GTE with Nikki and Joe Stiley.

"Nikki was on a plane that crashed," Frank told him. "Some people are in the Potomac River. I don't know if she made it."

Felch turned pale as the blood drained from his face.

Schneider brought a television set into the office, and the men sat and solemnly watched the news.

Chester Panzer cruised southbound on George Washington Memorial Parkway in the WJLA crew car back toward National Airport. Approaching the 14th Street Bridge spans, he and George Patterson saw flashing emergency lights to the left, off the other side of the road. There was nothing that looked like a plane crash, just a couple of emergency vehicles.

The men talked it over. *Is this what we're looking for? I don't know.* If they kept driving toward National Airport and had to circle back, they'd never make it with this traffic. They decided that they had better check it out.

Panzer parked beneath the 14th Street Bridge, sheltered from the snowfall. From the trunk of the crew car, Patterson lifted the bulky video recorder and carried it against his hip with the strap across his shoulders. Panzer carried the video camera, and the men trudged across the median through snowdrifts that were halfway to their knees.

People were clustered about five hundred feet away. Walking through the snowfield, the newsmen plugged in the cable between the camera and recorder. As they approached, a park police helicopter rose into view. Panzer hoisted the camera to his shoulder, brought his eye to the viewfinder, and hit the RECORD button.

Usher circled the helicopter low over the wreckage. He thought about how to pull off a rescue without putting any lives at risk. Eagle One's powerful rotor wash pummeled the survivors with chunks of ice and freezing water. Ice tumbled over the water.

Windsor dropped a rescue buoy to the victims in the water — the small plastic yellow ball that was designed to unfurl automatically when it hit water and inflate into a personal flotation device. But the buoy didn't inflate. The rotor wash blew it away from the victims, and it skittered across the ice.

Bert Hamilton swam over to Eagle One and, blood streaking down his face, grabbed on to one of the helicopter's skids. The sudden weight on the skid tipped the helicopter's center of gravity. Tilt too much and a rotor might strike the water. Usher gently guided the cyclic joystick to compensate for the shift in weight.

"Don't do that," Windsor yelled at Hamilton. "Wait a second."

Eagle One was not equipped for rescue: no hoist to lower down, no life vests, no useful equipment at all. All Windsor had at his disposal was the towline used to pull the helicopter trailer out of the hangar, a length of rope with a clip at one end. He attached the rope to the inside of the helicopter and tied a bowline knot in the free end, forming a loop.

Windsor wanted to tell Hamilton to put his foot in the loop and hold on to the rope, but it was impossible to speak over Eagle One's roaring engine. And by this time the crash survivors had been immersed in icy slush so long that their hands and feet no longer worked.

Hamilton took the rope and wrapped it around his waist. Usher slowly lifted him from the water and sidled Eagle One to shore.

The National Airport ambulance was parked near the edge of the bluff, with first responders and bystanders gathered around, in the vicinity of a small tree that was too close for comfort. Usher needed room to safely bring Eagle One close enough to hand off Hamilton. He toggled the helicopter's speaker and said to move the ambulance back.

Harris pulled the ambulance away while a group of firefighters tackled the tree, whose trunk was a few inches in diameter, snapping it to the ground and tossing it to the side to create a small zone for Eagle One. A group of first responders and bystanders grabbed Hamilton as Eagle One approached, hustled him over to a gurney, wrapped him in a blanket, and carried him to the back of the ambulance.

Inside the back of National Airport's ambulance, paramedic Ed Smith began to assess Hamilton's injuries with an external head-to-toe examination.

"One down, five to go," Usher said to Windsor, circling back out to the shattered ice.

Engine 16 was among the fire department vehicles merging toward the 14th Street Bridge. Trucks drove against traffic in the opposing lanes and cut across the National Mall. Cars were a constant obstacle. John Leck and the other firefighters had to repeatedly hop off the running board and push vehicles out of the way.

At the ramp to the HOV span of the 14th Street Bridge, Engine 16 could go no farther. Traffic was completely halted and had nowhere to go. Dean ordered his firefighters to walk the rest of the way to the scene.

More Washington fire department vehicles arrived at the scene, clustering on the HOV bridge. One driver used the grille of a pumper to push the Jersey barrier out of the way so vehicles and personnel could get to the other side of the bridge.

Also on their way to the Potomac were five ambulances from Prince George's County, five ambulances from Montgomery County, and a rescue squad from Fairfax County with a team of divers.

4:25 P.M.

Arlington County firefighters worked to extricate two critically injured men on the 14th Street Bridge. The cars of Ray Bowles and Lieutenant Michael Saunders had been mangled by the left wing and landing gear of Flight 90. Both men had sustained severe upper-body injuries. Firefighters used a Hurst Jaws of Life hydraulic tool to peel away the roof and pry open the doors of their cars. An Arlington County ambulance parked next to Saunders's Renault was ready to take the men to the hospital.

District of Columbia deputy fire chief Thomas O'Connell arrived and announced that by the authority of the mayor of Washington, he was commanding officer in charge of the Flight 90 crash scene. He told Arlington County crews to stop what they were doing.

By law, the boundary of the District of Columbia includes the Potomac River up to the waterline on the Virginia side. Washington claims the portion of the 14th Street Bridge over water, while the portion over land is the jurisdiction of authorities in Virginia. Because the crash occurred over water, primary responsibility for managing the incident clearly belonged to DC.

O'Connell told Arlington County fire chief Thomas Hawkins to get his crew off the bridge. His men would take it from here.

Saunders was placed in the DC Fire Department's Medic 5. John Brazier worked on the severely injured man during transport to the closest hospital in Washington, Georgetown University Hospital, 3.6 miles away.

At the Federal Triangle station, a few more riders squeezed into train 410. The next stop was the Smithsonian station on the other side of the National Mall.

Michael Greene, the operator of train 410, brought the subway to a halt at the Smithsonian Interlocking as directed by rail supervisor Davis. Taking the train out of automatic mode, Greene switched it to manual operation.

Davis told Greene to proceed through the red signal across the interlocking. Greene advanced the train up to around fifteen miles per hour, but halfway through the interlocking, it began to shift inadvertently over to the southbound tracks.

"Hey, Greene, hold up," Davis said into his radio.

"Hold up," the train operator replied.

"Greene, hold up!" Davis barked.

"Roger."

Greene stopped the train before more than a couple of cars were switched over to the parallel track. The rail supervisor walked around the front of train 410 to size up the situation.

"Central," Davis said on his radio.

"Yes, sir," Banks replied from the OCC.

"This, ah, this switch doesn't look right," Davis said. "I'm going to pull the train back and try again."

Davis walked the length of the train to the operator's compartment at the far end.

The DC Fire Department established a command post on the 14th Street Bridge. Arlington County Fire Department withdrew its personnel from the bridge and set up a staging area next to the Potomac. From this point onward, the District of Columbia fire, police, and medical examiner assumed the lead for the Flight 90 crash response.

Five army UH-1 helicopters from Fort Belvoir arrived at National Airport, landing in a row on the tarmac. The tower asked Usher whether a Huey should join the rescue. One of the military helicopters could hold a dozen passengers. Usher advised them to stand by; there wasn't enough room between the spans for more than one helicopter. Besides, he reasoned, the Huey's more powerful prop wash might swamp the weakened and injured victims.

Tethered to each other by a six-foot video recorder cable, Patterson and Panzer moved together like a well-practiced dance duo at the top of the bank overlooking the Potomac. Panzer aimed his lens on the action happening in front of them, where rescuers and bystanders gathered, while Patterson kept an eye out to make sure nobody tripped or got in the way.

Usher took Eagle One back out and hovered over the wreckage. Of the five victims in the water, Windsor assessed one of them — Arland Williams — as in the worst shape. He was in water up to his shoulders and bleeding from the head. Windsor dropped the tow rope to Williams, who handed it to the others.

With hands that were badly injured and numbed from the cold, none of the survivors in the water thought they could hang on to a rope. Flight attendant Kelly Duncan took the rope under her right arm, then wrapped it across her chest and around her left arm.

Usher deftly twisted the collective and nudged the cyclic joystick to gently lift Duncan from the water. She barely held on, keeping the rope tucked under her left arm by pressing tightly against her ribs. Duncan dangled shoeless in the air, her uniform torn and pantyhose shredded with holes.

Eagle One sidled to the shore. As the helicopter approached the riverbank, three civilian bystanders stepped into the frigid water up their knees to grab Duncan and hand her over to firefighters standing in the snow.

Firefighters carried Duncan to a waiting gurney and wrapped her in a blanket. She was taken to National Airport's ambulance and placed next to Bert Hamilton in back.

Windsor told Usher that rescuing the victims one at a time was taking too long. The victims had been in the water for almost a half hour and were getting weak; they were going to lose them.

"Give us another rope," Usher said over the helicopter's speaker.

Firefighters handed Windsor a life ring on a rope. Usher rotated Eagle One and headed out over the water.

4:28 P.M.

Rail supervisor James Davis walked the length of train 410 and climbed up the end door of the last car. Entering the operator's compartment, Davis told Greene to remove his key from the console so he could take over operation of the train from his end.

"I'm going to try to pull it back into the station and clear that sig-switch," Davis said to Greene over his radio. "Let me know when we're clear."

Operating the controls manually, Davis drove the train slowly backward.

As the final car was leaving the crossover, one set of wheels rolled back onto the northbound track, but the second set — at what had been the front of the train — remained on the southbound rails.

The train reversed while straddling two sets of parallel tracks. One of the wheels skipped out of the track, derailing the train. The last car was dragged diagonally toward a foot-thick concrete wall where the crossover split into two separate tunnels.

Unlike the heavyweight steel railcars and streetcars of yesteryear, carriage bodies for modern mass transit systems such as the WMATA and Bay Area Rapid Transit are fabricated with extruded aluminum beams and parts. A modern subway car is strongest along its axis, offering the greatest protection from a collision from the front or rear. While an upright aluminum soda can will support a lot of weight, the container will crush easily if squeezed from the sides.

The company that fabricated the WMATA and BART subway cars never took a lateral or side-rake collision into account in their designs, and never tested a prototype for crashworthiness in a side impact.

From the operator's compartment at the far end, Davis felt a jerking motion as the train rolled backward and ground to a halt. Suddenly he lost propulsion, braking, and the train's electrical system.

Arthur Hastings, a fifty-year-old businessman from Bowie,

Maryland, was aboard train 410 with his wife, Marion. He watched the horror unfold in slow motion as the concrete wall inched closer until it crunched into the side of the car.

The concrete edge cut into the carriage just behind the rear sliding doors, ripping a fifteen-foot gash and shattering windows, slicing into the packed passenger compartment like a dull knife. The car groaned and creaked with metal bending and twisting. Handrails and seats were shoved aside by the concrete wedge impaling the carriage, forcing riders into a tangled pile in the rear of the car. Sharp pain pierced Ruby Mae Thomas's legs and left shoulder as she was violently jostled.

The floor heaved upward, slamming passengers' heads into the ceiling, and then split open and dumped people onto the tracks. Mary O'Meara, sitting next to Thomas, toppled into the gap and was pinched against the concrete wall. Marion Hastings slipped out of her husband's hand and fell through the ruptured floor onto the tracks.

The concrete tore into the car's battery compartment, knocking out the train's electrical system. The ventilation system stopped and overhead lights went out, and then the emergency lights over the exits flickered off, plunging the train into darkness.

4:30 P.M.

As is routine following aviation incidents, the FAA closed National Airport to air traffic. Planes that were in transit to Washington National were redirected to Dulles International Airport in the Virginia suburbs.

Among those whose planes were diverted by the emergency were FAA administrator J. Lynn Helms, Secretary of the Interior James Watt, and Lady Bird Johnson, who was arriving for a social event.

At Tampa International Airport, relatives and friends waiting for the arrival of Flight 90 were escorted into Air Florida's VIP lounge and informed of the crash. It would be hours yet before they would know whether there were survivors.

Eagle One coasted back out to the hole in the ice and hovered above four survivors in the water. Once again, Windsor dropped the towline to Arland Williams.

Grab the rope, damn it, grab the rope, Windsor said to himself.

Instead, Williams handed the rope to Nikki Felch. Felch had watched Duncan being carried away by Eagle One and doubted she'd be able to maintain her hold on the rope while being lifted from the water; she had lost just about all use of her hands. Joe Stiley took the life ring and, with fractured bones in his hands and arms, managed to get his head and left shoulder through the ring and his arm cradled around Priscilla Tirado. They would be rescued together.

Usher kept Eagle One low above the water and delicately pulled all three toward the shore. Felch quickly lost her grip on the tow rope, as she'd expected, and dropped into the water. Kept afloat with a yellow life vest around her neck,

Priscilla Tirado, Joe Stiley, and Nikki Felch cling to ropes dangling from Eagle One.
Charles Pereira/Associated Press

she crossed her arms and floated on her back. Now that a helicopter was rescuing them, she knew could wait another minute or two.

Dragged through the water by Eagle One, Stiley and Tirado were pulled into slabs of ice stacked up near the shoreline by the helicopter's powerful rotor wash. Straining to keep ahold of Tirado as they plowed through the ice, Stiley was knocked in the ribs. Tirado tumbled from his

Eagle One hovers above as first responders retrieve Joe Stiley from the Potomac while Priscilla Tirado remained stranded in the water. Charles Pereira/Associated Press

weak embrace and was left stranded on a floe about forty feet from shore.

Firefighters stepped into the water to grab Stiley as Eagle One brought him close. "There's a man trapped out there," he told them. "He can't get himself out. You're going to have to go in and get him."

Hustling Stiley to the one ambulance that had driven to the river's edge, first responders found it full with two stretcher patients and Roger Olian, who had walked over from the jeep to be assessed by paramedic Ed Smith.

More medic units were needed immediately. Several other ambulances from Arlington and Washington were on the 14th Street Bridge, but since the other fire departments used different radio frequencies, there was no way to contact them and let them know they were needed.

Smith made a quick decision to remove the stretchers and place the victims directly on the cabin floor of the ambulance, laying Stiley next to Bert Hamilton and Kelly Duncan.

Priscilla Tirado floundered supine on a sheet of ice, weakened and delirious from hypothermia. She feebly paddled her arms in the air, unaware that she was no longer in the water.

Standing on the bank above the Potomac, Panzer zoomed the camera in close on Tirado's ashen face. Futilely writhing on the ice, her eyes wide in terror, Tirado seemed to look directly at Panzer through the camera lens and pleaded, "Help me."

My God, she's dying right in front of us, Panzer thought, pulling away from the camera viewfinder in horror. *I can't just stand here and watch.*

Patterson noticed his partner hesitate. "Stay focused," he told Panzer. "You have a job to do."

Panzer looked around. *There are people doing everything they can*, he reasoned. *What can I do?* Panzer took a deep breath and returned his eye to the viewfinder.

Windsor repeatedly dropped the life ring near Tirado, who didn't see it within easy reach next to her head. She'd lost awareness of her surroundings, expending the last of her body's energy on sheer survival. Her hands and fingers no longer functioned, as useless as wooden paddles. Grabbing the ring was impossible.

Like playing a carnival fishing game, Windsor dangled the life ring in an attempt to snag Tirado's arm. On his third try, Tirado hooked her forearm through the ring. With the most tenuous of holds, Usher pulled Tirado toward shore.

After she'd drifted only a few feet, Tirado's arm slipped from the life ring. Depleted of her adrenaline-fueled reserves, she rolled onto her back and began to slip beneath the surface of the water.

On the riverbank, firefighters were tying a rope around firefighter John Leck's waist to prepare him to wade into the water. One of the rules taught in rescue courses is never to go into cold or swiftly moving water without being tied off with a lifeline.

Standing with first responders, Lenny Skutnik was close enough to see the expression on Tirado's face. He was certain she was going to die. It was too much to take. He whipped off his jacket and Timex wristwatch, pulled off his boots, and pushed through a knot of firefighters to dive into the Potomac.

In four strong strokes of his arms, Skutnik reached Tirado as her head was going under water. He lifted her head out of the water, shoved her toward shore, and swam alongside her until John Leck waded out to grab Tirado.

"I have her now," he told Skutnik. "I have her."

Lifting her by her arms and legs, firefighters carried Tirado up the riverbank and dragged her along the ground, her bare abdomen on the snow, to the National Airport ambulance. The only place for her in the patient compartment was on top of the other survivors.

Despite a comparatively brief exposure to the intensely cold water, Leck emerged drained of strength and frozen to the core. Firefighters pulled Skutnik from the water. Staggering up the riverbank, Skutnik gathered his jacket and boots and joined Roger Olian and the others in the ambulance.

He never found his wristwatch, lost somewhere in the snow beside the Potomac.

4:33 P.M.

Mystified by the sudden shutdown of the train, Davis tried reaching Greene over the radio but received no response. The disruption of the train's electrical system had knocked out the train operator's radio. Greene could not contact the OCC and let them know there had been a derailment. The train's public address system was also disabled, so Greene couldn't provide any information to passengers.

Davis left the operator's compartment and walked the length of the train to investigate the issue further.

Terry Rylick was a plainclothes transit police officer assigned to patrol WMATA buses. He was aboard train 410 on his way to a police station when it derailed. Standing near the operator's compartment at the front of the wrecked carriage, neither he nor Greene was immediately aware that people were injured.

Rylick worked his way through the dark, tightly crowded carriage and discovered the enormity of the situation. The subway car had split wide open, nearly cut in half. Many people were hurt, and some were trapped.

The officer returned to Greene in the operator's compartment and told him that EMS was needed immediately. Greene's radio was inoperable, and Rylick could only communicate with the WMATA transit police department dispatcher. He could not talk with the OCC, which used a different radio frequency.

Rylick notified the police dispatcher of the emergency. The police dispatch office had a staffer walk to the OCC, located in a different part of the WMATA headquarters, because the direct "hotline" phone between the OCC and transit police was out of order.

Two survivors remained in the water. Nikki Felch floated on her back with her arms clenched across her chest. Usher led Eagle One out over the river and hovered above her. Windsor dropped the towline to Felch. "Hold the rope," he told her.

"I can't," she said to Windsor. Her hands were not capable of grasping anything.

"I have to go get her," the rescue technician told Usher, unbuckling his seat restraints.

Windsor was close to breaking one of the cardinal rules of emergency services: *Don't make things worse.* First responders should never put themselves in danger, or else an incident with one victim becomes an incident with two or more victims.

If he didn't break the rule outright, Windsor bent it to an extreme. He slid open the side door of the helicopter, scooted out, and stood on the skid. Without any restraint or tether, Windsor braced himself by pushing his lower back against the deck. Nothing attached him to the helicopter except the radio cable plugged into his helmet.

Usher weighed the risks: If Windsor fell, their problems would be exponentially compounded. There would be one more person in the water, with nobody in the helicopter to rescue them. And Usher would be called upon to explain to superiors why he'd allowed a member of his crew to fall out of his aircraft.

Please don't fall, Usher said to himself.

As a helicopter pilot in Vietnam, Usher had flown plenty of combat missions in dicey situations. He was confident of his ability to pull this off.

Usher brought Eagle One in very low, skimming the surface of the water, running alongside Felch with the skid inches away from her head. She extended her arm to Windsor. He reached down and grasped Felch's arm with one hand, and with the other grabbed the back of her collar. The shifting weight made the helicopter tilt, dipping the skids into the water. If a skid were snagged on ice or debris, it could be disastrous for all of them.

"Don, my feet are getting wet," Windsor said calmly.

Usher twisted the collective enough to raise Eagle One out of the water. Felch hitched her left knee over the toe

US Park Police rescue technician Gene Windsor grips Nikki Felch while standing untethered on the skid of Eagle One. Charles Pereira/Associated Press

of Windsor's boot. Usher kept the helicopter close to the water in case either of them fell. Windsor gripped her collar tightly as Eagle One coasted to rescuers waiting at the top of the riverbank.

Panzer recorded as Eagle One approached the shore with Felch dangling from the skid, hovering low with the rotors inches above the heads of rescuers. Eagle One was so low, Panzer was concerned that people were about to be decapitated. But Usher's adroit piloting skills brought the helicopter in safely for Felch to be handed off to firefighters.

Howard Piansky, along with another Arlington County firefighter and civilian bystander, carried Felch to the National Airport ambulance. They lost their hold on Felch and dropped her to the ground while a brief conversation transpired at the ambulance door.

There was no more room, Piansky was told. An ambulance is designed to accommodate one patient. A second stretcher patient can be strapped to the bench along the other side in a pinch. National's ambulance had four of the survivors laid out on the floor, as well as Roger Olian and Lenny Skutnik, and the paramedic Ed Smith. The ambulance was already beyond capacity. There was simply no more space for another patient to sit or lie down.

Thinking quickly, firefighters rushed Felch to a WMATA bus on the HOV bridge. She was placed by the heating vent and covered with jackets while Piansky assessed her injuries.

Eagle One flew once more to the Air Florida 90 debris in the middle of the Potomac. By the time they returned to the fragment of fuselage where the others had been, Arland Williams was gone. The fuselage had rotated and settled in the water, pulling him beneath the surface. Usher circled for a few minutes, searching the water and wreckage. Nothing.

Windsor looked desperately for any sign of Williams

beneath the surface of the water. He would have gone in after him. He knew that people can be resuscitated after thirty minutes or more in cold water. Windsor held back tears. He was crushed. *We were so close to saving them all,* he said to himself. *Could we have done anything differently?*

Usher flew Eagle One over the ice to make sure nothing was overlooked. The body of a male passenger had been ejected over the ice halfway across the river, with obviously fatal injuries. Another body had been thrown under the HOV bridge, also clearly dead.

Returning to shore, Usher spoke to rescuers over Eagle One's speaker. "That's all of them," he said. "There is nobody else alive out there."

During the entire rescue, Eagle One was never more than ten feet over the water. Most of the time, Usher flew the helicopter at an altitude between two and five feet.

4:35 P.M.

Davis, the rail supervisor, discovered why the train had stopped so suddenly when he reached the last car and saw the magnitude of the damage. He keyed his walkie-talkie and notified the OCC.

"This is Unit 31," Davis said. "We have got a derailment."

"What's your track?" Banks asked from the OCC. "On track 1?"

"We crossed over and got both tracks blocked," Davis said. "You may need to send an ambulance."

"Ambulance? You have injured passengers? Is that it?"

"I'm going to have to try to unload the train," Davis said. "I got . . . I got passengers hurt."

The OCC did not immediately respond to Davis's request to evacuate passengers.

The WMATA didn't want passengers leaving trains on their own through emergency exits. Metrorail trains didn't have instructions posted on how to exit in an emergency. The lever to manually open the sliding doors was hidden behind an unlabeled panel. The carriages weren't even equipped with emergency exit windows that popped out.

If a train was disabled, the WMATA's plan was for passengers to remain on board until they could be safely evacuated by personnel. Metrorail's plan to evacuate a train, should it be necessary, was to pull another train up to the front or back so passengers could safely step from one car to another. Alternatively, another train could be pulled up alongside and riders could step through aligned doorways. The agency never envisioned that passengers would need to exit a train in the middle of a tunnel and walk to a station.

Metrorail operated under the presumption that posting emergency exit instructions would invite mischief. Unruly passengers might try to open the doors and disrupt train operations. Somebody could get hurt if a door or window were opened while a train was moving.

Posting information about how to exit the train would expose passengers to the third rail, electrified with 750 volts, which would instantly kill anybody who came in contact with it. By the calculations of WMATA management, the hazard posed by posting emergency exit directions outweighed the benefit.

Davis told Rylick to walk the length of the train and tell passengers to remain on board until they could be evacuated in an orderly fashion.

4:36 P.M.

Usher landed Eagle One in a clear area on the damaged 14th Street Bridge and remained in the pilot's seat while Windsor went to look for the scene commander. The park police officers were still operating under the mistaken assumption that other survivors had made their way to shore and were prepared to medevac victims to MedStar Washington Hospital Center or Shock Trauma in Baltimore. Windsor wandered around looking for a fire department officer or anybody in charge who could provide information.

The scene on the bridge was disorganized and chaotic. There were scores of people in helmets of many colors, but nobody could tell Windsor who was in command. Windsor got back into Eagle One, and they returned to the Eagle's Nest.

One of the army's UH-1 helicopters standing by at National Airport was summoned to the 14th Street Bridge. Felch was carried from the WMATA bus to the helicopter and flown to MedStar.

The National Airport ambulance with the other Flight 90 victims didn't go to MedStar — the regional trauma center prepared for and expecting them — but to the smaller community hospital, National Hospital for Orthopaedics and Rehabilitation.

MedStar had been receiving bits and pieces of incomplete and incorrect secondhand information. Frustrated hospital officials called the fire department and news stations trying to learn about the unprecedented simultaneous disasters. Based on Usher's mistaken observation at the scene, Dr. William Fouty, chief of surgery at MedStar, was told that as many as forty people had been pulled from the Potomac.

Doctors at MedStar Washington Hospital Center heard from unofficial channels that two helicopters were headed their way with three or four victims from the Flight 90 crash. Medical staff were bewildered when only one helicopter arrived, with Nikki Felch.

National Hospital for Orthopaedics and Rehabilitation hadn't been officially notified, either, but had heard through the grapevine to expect as many as forty-five victims.

The patient care compartment of the National Airport ambulance reeked of jet fuel. Ed Smith moved gingerly to assess his patients while not stepping on the row of Flight 90 victims stacked like cordwood across the floor.

Warmed by the ambulance's heating system, blood vessels that had been clamped down by hypothermia began to dilate and restore circulation to the muscles and skin. The victims began shivering. Blood started to seep from numerous superficial cuts and abrasions and mix with the water pooling on the floor of the ambulance. As circulation returned, so did sensation, and the injured moaned in pain.

Skutnik had been running on adrenaline since leaping off the riverbank. He had been so jacked and focused on Tirado that he didn't notice the frigid temperature of the Potomac. It was while crouching inside the ambulance, his nerves settling back to normal, that the deep cold set in and Skutnik began shivering uncontrollably along with the others.

Seeing Joe Stiley in so much worse shape, chattering and bleeding on the floor, Skutnik covered him with his jacket. Stiley needed it more.

"How long until we get to a hospital," Tirado asked.

"Just a few minutes," Smith told her.

Olian tried to buoy spirits in the ambulance by telling Kelly Duncan he'd take her out for lunch when this was all over.

One resource Washington had in abundance was media. Print and broadcast news organizations from major cities across the country and around the world had representatives in the capital. When news of Flight 90 broke, reporters flocked to the story. Each of the major networks, the three local news stations, radio networks, and wire services sent representatives to the 14th Street Bridge.

The open-floor newsroom of the Scripps-Howard Washington Bureau was a hive of activity. Reporters worked the phones while listening to news of the Flight 90 crash on the radio. Susan Bennett, Washington correspondent for the *Philadelphia Daily News*, received a call from her editor at the paper. We want a story about the plane crash, she was told.

Bennett covered the Washington scene for the tabloid and didn't usually report on breaking news. But this was huge, her biggest story since Elvis died when she was United Press International bureau chief in Memphis. There hadn't been a fatal airliner crash in the United States in more than two years. Bennett leaped at the chance.

"Let's go to the 14th Street Bridge," she told a colleague.

"We can't get there," he replied.

"We have to try," Bennett said.

She grabbed a few things from her desk — money, pens, and her press identification. Fortunately, she'd worn a down jacket to work and clunky winter boots instead of the dressier shoes she ordinarily wore.

The McPherson Square Metro station was only three blocks from the Scripps-Howard office at Vermont and L Street. Taking the Blue/Orange subway to the Smithsonian station would get them halfway to the 14th Street Bridge.

Bennett and her colleague descended into the McPherson Square station and found a train waiting with is doors open. The reporters squeezed into the packed train car. But the doors didn't shut behind them. Instead, riders were told that the subway was closed.

Cursing the Metro, the reporters ran up an out-of-order escalator back to the ground level on 14th Street. The bridge was about two miles to the south down the street. They began running down the sidewalk, alongside the White House, past the Smithsonian Metro station where the derailment was evolving beneath their feet, and across the National Mall past the Washington Monument.

Along the way, the reporters attracted the interest of three teenagers who began jogging along with them. The teens didn't know where they were running to, or why. The group trotted down 14th Street past the Bureau of Engraving, bounding through snowdrifts and scaling Jersey barriers.

A police officer blocked their path on the 14th Street Bridge. The bridge is closed, he told them. You can't get across.

Bennett stepped back and looked around. The police had opened one lane of traffic to allow vehicles still on the HOV bridge to continue slowly to the Virginia side. She saw a van in line and went to speak with the driver.

"Would you let us ride with you to the other end of the bridge?" Bennett asked.

"Sure, get in," he said.

"We have three friends with us," she said. "Is there room for them, too?"

"Sure," he said.

The five piled into the van and crawled past the police undisturbed. Once at the Virginia side of the bridge, Bennett and her colleague thanked the van driver, bid farewell to their young traveling companions, and dashed to the riverside to find witnesses and first responders to interview. Among those Bennett interviewed loitering on the 14th Street Bridge overlooking the crash site was Jack Sexton, a bartender from Alexandria.

After spending some time at the Potomac, Bennett

learned that press and emergency personnel were at the Twin Bridges Marriott. The reporter walked through snow halfway up to the knee, arriving at the hotel chilled to the core. Her feet were frozen and numb. She took off her boots and joined other reporters and firefighters warming their feet in the hotel's heated pool.

4:38 P.M.

OCC supervisor Kenneth Banks used a dedicated phone line to notify the fire department communications center.

"We need an ambulance down here between Smithsonian and Federal Triangle stations," Banks said. "There is an interlocking with approximately a thousand feet between each station. We have a train that is derailed there."

"Oh, come on, you're kidding," the fire department watch commander responded.

"No, I am not kidding," Banks said. "We got some people injured. We don't know how many at this time."

The watch commander transferred the call to Steve Souder.

"We need an ambulance down between Smithsonian and Federal Triangle stations," Banks repeated. "A train has derailed there."

"A train derailed and people are injured?" Souder asked.

"Yes," Banks said.

"Okay, boss," Souder said. "We'll do the best we can."

Unclear about the nature of the subway incident, the

District of Columbia Fire Department dispatched two engines to the Federal Triangle Metro station. The derailment was in the same fire department response zone as the 14th Street Bridge, and nearly all apparatuses were already occupied at the Flight 90 crash scene. The engines sent to the Metro would have to be sent from more distant stations.

In the meantime, passengers aboard train 410 were told nothing. They waited in the darkness, packed in carriages that were becoming stifling, unaware that the delay was anything other than routine. Some told jokes. While those in the crashed subway car were either dead, injured, or traumatized, many of those on the rest of the train wouldn't even learn that their train had derailed until they arrived home and watched the news.

An Air Florida pickup truck pulled up on the ramp to the 14th Street Bridge, and two men exited the vehicle. Kenneth Madden, one of the ranking police officers on the scene, wanted to know why the men were present at a crash scene that was still active. In the bed of the truck, Madden saw tarpaulins and buckets of paint, presumably to obscure Air Florida markings and prevent them from appearing in the media.

"That's evidence," Madden said, pointing to the shards of debris strewn across the water. "If you touch anything, you're going to jail."

The men got back in the truck and left the area.

4:45 P.M.

Plainclothes officer Terry Rylick informed the WMATA police dispatcher of the gravity of the situation in the tunnel. "There are people hurt," he said. "One woman is trapped between the train and the wall."

Aboard the remainder of the train, riders were getting restless. They'd been packed tightly together, most of them standing, in the darkness for fifteen minutes. Nobody had provided any information about the cause for the delay or how long it would be, and for some, conditions inside the airless and oppressively warm train were becoming intolerable. A few passengers kicked out windows and jumped down to the tracks or exited the end door and made their way along the tracks to a Metro station.

Sparks flew out from beneath the derailed train car. Davis got on his radio and told the OCC to turn off the electrified third rail. Anybody touching it would be instantly killed.

"Roger," he was told.

The OCC never turned off the third rail. Personnel in the OCC were in crisis, dealing with a sudden disruption of Metrorail during the peak ridership period. Banks was the only person in the OCC handling the radio for the entire system, and he was being bombarded with problem reports.

Metrorail superintendent Joseph Taylor and assistant superintendent Paul Hobgood were under tremendous pressure to move thousands of commuters to their destinations. They were preoccupied with the thirty-five to forty thousand riders in the Metro subway system at that very moment. Trains needed to be off-loaded at stations and buses arranged to re-route around the sudden yawning transit gap.

Taylor's shift ended at 4:00 P.M., after which assistant superintendent Paul Hobgood was supposed to take over supervision of the OCC. Taylor was sticking around because of the unusual circumstances and assumed that Hobgood was in charge now. Hobgood assumed that Taylor was in charge because Taylor was still the boss.

In fact, nobody was in charge. Nobody assumed command of the derailment. Nobody was coordinating with the fire department and police. Nobody was responsible for ensuring that the thirteen hundred passengers on train 410 were safely escorted out of the tunnel.

An evacuation could have begun. Five WMATA supervisors and rail employees were at the Federal Triangle station, but passengers were kept aboard train 410 because nobody was authorized to begin its evacuation.

4:50 P.M.

The National Airport ambulance pulled up to the emergency department door of National Hospital for Orthopaedics and Rehabilitation. Gurneys were brought out to the ambulance to carry the four Flight 90 survivors, while Lenny Skutnik and Roger Olian walked in unassisted.

The patients were given armbands that identified them by number because none of them were carrying identification. They would remain numbers until they could be interviewed later and provide information.

When the blanket was unwrapped from Joe Stiley, clumps of ice stuck to his clothing. The body temperatures of the survivors were too low to register on rectal thermometers, which go down to ninety degrees Fahrenheit. Priscilla Tirado was the most critical of the group, with a fracture of the left femur and a core body temperature of eighty-one degrees, well into the danger zone.

The survivors were rapidly rewarmed to treat severe hypothermia. They were wrapped in heated electric blankets. Nurses put masks on them so they could breathe warmed, humidified air. Heat was applied internally by instilling warm fluid into the stomach through a nasogastric tube, and by placing a needle through the abdominal wall to allow warm fluid to bathe the abdominal cavity.

The survivors were barely conscious in the emergency department, so deeply in shock that they felt nothing while the orthopedic surgeon reset their bones. Once they were stabilized, Joe Stiley underwent surgery for fractures of his left leg, and Bert Hamilton to repair his fractured right arm.

By one of several fortuitous coincidences on January 13, none of the Flight 90 survivors had injuries that exceeded the capabilities of National Hospital for Orthopaedics and Rehabilitation.

Roger Olian and Lenny Skutnik were examined and placed in warm showers while their clothes were dried in the hospital's laundry department. When Olian's hands and feet warmed up, they began to hurt excruciatingly. The hospital asked Olian to stay the night for observation, but he declined.

When Tirado regained alertness, the doctor asked her name.

"Prissy," she replied. "Where is my baby?"

Medical staff held off on telling her the terrible news about her husband and child until family could be by her side for support. Tirado drifted in and out of consciousness all night.

Duncan felt tremendous guilt for surviving the crash while others did not. She felt that she had failed her duty to her passengers, and cried for hours. "I let people down," she told a nurse. "I could have saved somebody."

At MedStar Washington Hospital Center, Nikki Felch was found to have broken bones in her right leg and right arm, a scalp laceration, rib fractures, and a collapsed lung. Her respiratory system was inflamed from inhaling jet fuel.

James Davis and Terry Rylick, along with an attendant from the Federal Triangle station, began to evacuate riders from train 410.

Metrorail trains were equipped with a two-piece wooden ladder stowed under a seat at the front of the car. When assembled, the ladder would be about four feet long and was designed to allow riders to step down from the end of the car to the track level. Nothing secured the ladder to the train.

The end doors of the derailed subway car were inaccessible. When the ladder was placed against a side door, it was too long and unstable. Davis dispensed with the ladder and assisted passengers down to the track.

Passengers followed in line along a three-foot-wide catwalk to the Federal Triangle Metro station.

4:53 P.M.

The first fire department vehicle to arrive at the Federal Triangle Metro station, Engine 3, pulled up in front of the curved marble facade on the 300 block of 12th Street NW, between Pennsylvania Avenue and the Mall.

Firefighters walked through stone arches to a plaza at the neck of the hourglass-shaped building, then down a flight of stairs to the station. Hundreds of people were wandering in and out of the station, unaware of an emergency.

The station attendant opened a passage to allow the firefighters to bypass the fare gates. A steady stream of passengers walked past them as they descended another set of stairs to a long platform between two sets of tracks. Firefighters walked to the southern end of the platform, down steps to the track, and then 150 feet to the site of the derailment.

In boots and full turnout gear, the walk from the curb to the scene took twenty-one minutes.

Arriving at the interlocking, firefighters found train 410 being evacuated by a Metrorail supervisor and a police officer. There was a sense of weary frustration among riders, but no expression of alarm. Since most passengers had no idea there had been a fatal incident, panic began to filter through the crowd only when firefighters unexpectedly appeared wearing face masks.

At the back of the train, firefighters found an unimaginable scene. The last car looked like it had been struck by another train and smashed against the concrete pillar, split open and crushed. One end of the car was a jumble of bent and twisted metal that entrapped several people, living and dead. More than twenty people were injured.

Engine 3's officer in charge quickly realized the magnitude of the crash. This was a major incident that required more resources immediately — more firefighters, more EMTs, and most of all rescue tools: metal-cutting tools, saws, the Hurst Jaws of Life, generators, and lights. But three of the city's four rescue squads were already in service on the 14th Street Bridge.

Headquarters urgently needed to be notified. But the firefighters' radios did not work in Metrorail's tunnels. As a cost-saving measure, antennas that would carry the fire radio signal underground had been eliminated from the Metrorail design. The officer in charge had to ask the transit police officer to contact his dispatcher and relay a message to the fire department by telephone.

District of Columbia Fire dispatched four engines, two trucks, two battalion commanders, and a unit carrying breathing and salvage gear to the Federal Triangle and Smithsonian Metro stations.

James E. Burnett was still new to the job, still learning how things worked around the office. Burnett was one of five members of the National Transportation Safety Board (NTSB), an independent federal agency that investigates incidents involving aviation, rail transportation, commercial trucking, and pipelines.

Burnett had been with the NTSB less than a month, having been nominated by President Reagan and confirmed by the Senate for a five-year term. Prior to joining the agency, Burnett had no experience in aviation or any technical subject. He was a practicing attorney and judge from Arkansas. His area of expertise was jurisprudence.

On the afternoon of January 13, Burnett was in a two-hour briefing about how the NTSB investigated aviation incidents. The board had a "Go Team" ready to rush to the scene of an accident twenty-four hours a day. Working under the supervision of a board member, each team had a chief investigator and experts in areas such as weather, witness interviewing, aircraft maintenance, and other technical subjects.

After considering all the evidence developed in an investigation, the NTSB would issue a report of its conclusions. The agency has no say in penalties or sanctions, but acts as an impartial arbiter of facts in the pursuit of public safety.

Just after 4:00 P.M., during a budget conference, Frank Taylor, the agency's director of accident investigations, interrupted the meeting with news about the crash of Flight 90.

In many ways, the NTSB investigations of the Flight 90 crash and Metrorail derailment were unlike any in the agency's history. Never before had incidents happened so close to the agency's L'Enfant Plaza front door.

The investigation of Flight 90 began within seconds of the crash. Timothy Borson, a member of the NTSB's aviation Go Team, was approaching the 14th Street Bridge ramp heading to his home in Virginia when he heard about the plane crash on his CB radio. Borson left his car on the ramp and walked to the scene to begin interviewing witnesses and taking notes.

Francis McAdams, the board member in charge of the Flight 90 investigation, had already left work for the day when the crash happened. His car broke down while driving through northwest Washington. McAdams walked four miles through the snow the rest of the way home. A message from the office was waiting for him when he stepped through the door at 6:30 P.M. He immediately set out on the journey back into the city.

The person who was next in line as chief investigator for an aviation incident was inaccessible somewhere in the Metrorail system. Rudolf Kapustin, who was still at work, stepped up and began coordinating the investigation of Flight 90. His first act was to call National Airport and impound the deicing fluid used on the plane.

By the time Eagle One was dragging crash survivors from the Potomac, the NTSB's Go Team had set up a temporary command post in Hangar 6 at National Airport. Members of the team impounded maintenance records, flight logs, and other documents. Air traffic control personnel were interviewed. Technicians took samples from the fuel tanks used to top off Flight 90.

The next day, the NTSB moved its command center to

the Twin Bridges Marriott. Other groups participated: the FAA, Boeing, engine-maker Pratt & Whitney, Air Florida, and the Air Lines Pilots Association.

At around 4:40 P.M., Harold Storey, chief of the agency's railroad investigation branch, received a call informing him that a Metrorail train had derailed in the tunnel between the Smithsonian and Federal Triangle stations. Storey and Patricia Goldman, the NTSB board member in charge of the train 410 incident, went into the L'Enfant Plaza Metro station and walked through the tunnel to the scene to survey the situation while the evacuation was still under way and injured riders were still trapped aboard the train.

5:00 P.M.

At the Potomac, fire and rescue personnel debated whether people could still be alive in the Air Florida 90 cabin. They did not know whether any portion of the fuselage was intact underwater, possibly with survivors in an air bubble. Rescue efforts don't stop until it's known for certain that there is nobody to rescue.

It wasn't until divers could get close enough to visually confirm that the fuselage was broken into pieces that they determined there were no more survivors.

"I don't think we're going to get any more out alive," said James Trollinger, Arlington County's emergency services coordinator. Activity at the scene shifted from rescue to recovery.

Fire and rescue units from the District of Columbia and neighboring jurisdictions continued to pour into the Flight 90 crash scene as Washington fire officials ordered some of their own back to their stations or to the Metro derailment. The dozens of emergency vehicles around the Potomac and 14th Street Bridge complex formed a sea of flashing lights.

Arriving crews operated independently, joining a growing crowd of first responders doing very little. An ambulance from the Falls Church Volunteer Fire Department left the scene and went back into service while others were still responding to people injured in their vehicles on the 14th Street Bridge and the Metro derailment.

The all-volunteer Bethesda–Chevy Chase Rescue Squad sent five advanced life support ambulances and deputy fire chief Josh Vayer to the Potomac — the largest response of any neighboring jurisdiction. The Montgomery County Police cleared the intersections on Wisconsin Avenue all the way to the city line, allowing crews to make good time until they hit Washington.

Having traveled through the city together, all the Bethesda–Chevy Chase vehicles arrived at the 14th Street Bridge at the same time. Vayer was unable to locate a command post at the scene or anybody in charge. Attempting to contact their counterparts from Washington, personnel from Bethesda–Chevy Chase were unable to obtain any definitive information about where they should be or what they should be doing. After wandering around the scene for fifteen minutes, they learned that there were no more survivors and they were no longer needed.

At its peak, the District of Columbia Fire Department had thirty-seven vehicles and eighty-six personnel at the Flight 90 crash scene, along with those from Arlington, Alexandria, Fairfax, and Bethesda–Chevy Chase. More than two hundred first responders in all. They used nine different radio frequencies — none of which were in common among jurisdictions. Nobody could talk with one another.

First responders milled about with no direction or coordination. One fire official remarked that the Potomac was lined with "hundreds of authorized spectators in white hats" — officers who were just standing around doing nothing.

The fireboat arrived at the crash site far too late for rescue. Unsure of their location during the thick of the snowstorm, firefighters skating across the ice in National Airport's airboat stopped to get their bearings. The friction of the boat scraping against the ice warmed the rails on the hull. The momentary stop was long enough for ice beneath the airboat to melt and refreeze, firmly cementing the craft in place.

Abandoned and stranded vehicles were scattered around downtown streets and the ramps leading to the 14th Street Bridge, hindering access for the heavy equipment needed for the Flight 90 recovery effort. Thomas Downs, the city's transportation director, ordered all the city's tow trucks to tow any unattended vehicles in the vicinity of the 14th Street Bridge to the District of Columbia impound yard.

Among the vehicles towed away were the car of NTSB Go Team member Timothy Borson and Roger Olian's red Datsun pickup.

5:10 P.M.

Off-loading passengers from the derailed train shifted the weight of the car just enough to allow a piece of metal in the wreckage to contact the third rail, causing an explosion of sparks beneath the train. The third rail, still energized with 750 volts, posed a deadly hazard to passengers still trapped inside, those evacuating through the tunnel, and first responders.

Alarmed firefighters stopped the evacuation of passengers and told Davis to once again ask the OCC to shut off power to the third rail.

Traffic and the weather conspired against the DC Fire Department response to the Metro crash. A battalion chief arrived at the Federal Triangle station at 5:03, nearly a half hour after the call was received. The first ambulance didn't arrive until 5:14.

Communication was a persistent problem. Because the WMATA tunnels were not equipped with repeaters for fire department frequencies, information had to continue to be passed from the WMATA police officer or a rail supervisor to the OCC, and then to the fire department. Some responses came via couriers, firefighters who ran all the way to deliver commands verbally.

Despite being told of trapped victims at 4:40 P.M., fire officials didn't call for metal-cutting and other specialized extrication tools — some of which were already in use on the 14th Street Bridge to rescue victims from vehicles — until more than a half hour later.

At the request of the DC Fire Department, Bethesda–Chevy Chase Rescue Squad sent a heavy-duty rescue unit to the Federal Triangle station. Once on the scene, volunteers lugged the Hurst Jaws of Life, airbags, chocks, and other rescue equipment through the tunnel to the derailment site. None of it was needed.

Metal-cutting tools were used to extricate all the victims from the mangled subway car. One male passenger was compressed and trapped beneath two passengers who had been crushed to death.

Some remained on the derailed train by choice. Ruth Cannon stayed on the train to accompany her friend, Deborah Davis, who'd broken her right leg. Cannon had just run into Davis in a million-to-one coincidence at the Farragut West station. They hadn't seen each other since high school. Arthur Hastings wouldn't leave his wife, who also had a broken leg.

Hastings had formed a bond with Walter Samuel of Landover. Samuel hurt his neck when the subway car floor shoved him into the ceiling. The men exchanged phone numbers and promised to stay in touch. When it was time to part ways, Samuel said, "I'll see you soon, Arthur."

"You, too, Walter," Hastings said. "I'll see you soon."

Over the next two hours, ambulances from the District of Columbia and Bethesda–Chevy Chase Rescue Squad transported Metrorail victims to MedStar Washington Hospital Center, George Washington Hospital Center, and Howard University Hospital.

Because of the lack of communication and coordination, patients were not distributed in any rational way among hospitals in the city. Nineteen of the twenty-five people injured on the subway derailment were transported to MedStar, putting a heavy burden on the hospital's resources, while other equally capable departments received one or two patients and could have easily handled one or two more.

Had communications been better among the park police, National Airport, and the DC Fire Department, transport of the Metro injured could have been faster than ambulances navigating snowbound streets — the army helicopters standing by at National Airport could have ferried them to MedStar or Shock Trauma.

So many resources had been drawn to the Potomac River and the Metro derailment that for the second time in less than twenty-four hours, the DC Fire Department activated its Plan E, calling the next shift in early to ensure enough coverage in the District of Columbia for public safety.

Panzer and Patterson decided it was time to get the video of the incredible rescue that they just witnessed to WJLA. Panzer drove across the median and headed north on George Washington Memorial Parkway.

Patterson brought up the glitches they had with the equipment earlier in the day. Neither of them had seen the video that they had recorded. "What if something happened and we didn't get it?" he said to Panzer. "What if the cable was bad?"

"Don't even joke," Panzer said. "Don't talk about it or you'll jinx it."

Traffic on the parkway had eased, allowing them to make good time until crossing the Arlington Memorial Bridge. Entering the District of Columbia, Panzer hit a wall of traffic near the Lincoln Memorial. The rush-hour flow of vehicles going toward Virginia was still peaking. An immobile line of cars on Ohio Avenue went through the intersection, crossing their path and making any further progress impossible. It would take forever to get to the station.

Patterson contacted WJLA with the crew car's two-way radio. The news desk said that a news truck was setting up for a live segment remote in front of the Ellipse, about a mile away to the east. The mobile unit had equipment to transmit the video to the station.

It would be quicker to run to the truck than try to navigate one mile in downtown rush-hour traffic. Panzer handed the tape cassette to Patterson, who was a distance runner. "Take it and go," he said.

Patterson tucked the tape into his jacket and bounded through the snow to the WJLA mobile unit.

Hundreds of people gathered on the 14th Street Bridge and along the Potomac riverbank to watch activity at the crash site. Many of these spectators were later annoyed to discover that their cars had been towed to Washington's impound yard.

Volunteers poured in offering to help — nurses, doctors, Boy Scouts — adding to the general sense of disorder at the scene. At least two fake doctors were caught trying to insert themselves in the drama. Police put fencing along the George Washington Memorial Parkway to keep spectators and the press away.

For many who worked in Washington, there was no way home. With a paucity of information about which bridges were open or closed, drivers didn't know what route to take to Northern Virginia, further tangling traffic as drivers sought alternative ways home. Many drivers gave up in frustration and left their cars on the street. The Blue/Orange Line was inoperable, and with the HOV bridge closed there was no public transportation into Northern Virginia.

Thousands of workers were stranded in Washington. Hotels sold out throughout the city. Many filled bars and restaurants, watching the news on television.

Many commuters recall it took hours to get home that day.

6:03 P.M.

Panzer's tape had been edited and shared with the ABC network news division. Anchor Frank Reynolds interrupted broadcasts with a special report that included the first video from the scene. Panzer's stunning video was replayed on news broadcasts, and still images were used in news stories the next day around the world.

Videos of the crash scene and the rescue informed people, delivering good news and bad. Barbara Hamilton recognized the feet of her husband, Bert, as he was placed into the ambulance. He had big feet; she'd recognize them anywhere. Seeing those big shoes sticking out from the blanket told her that he'd somehow survived the crash.

Josephine Henrietta Mirrone, Priscilla Tirado's aunt, watched the rescue on television in her Wheaton, Maryland, home. When she heard about the crash of Flight 90, Mirrone called Tirado's stepmother, Caroline Keefer, in Clearwater.

"Was Priscilla on that plane?" Mirrone asked.

"Yes, they were on that flight," Keefer replied.

Mirrone watched the horrifying scene on the local news. A park police helicopter hovered above the iced-over Potomac. It didn't seem possible that anybody could have survived. She talked with Keefer while watching the rescue on television.

"My God," she exclaimed. "They just took Priscilla out of the water! I saw it on TV! She's alive! She's alive!"

Teresa Pringle thought the weather and traffic had delayed her husband's drive home from his job at Arlington National Cemetery. Joe Nathan Pringle, twenty-eight, was a mechanic who supervised a garage crew. When workers were let go early, Pringle and his crew left together in their cars. He was last in a caravan of coworkers driving over the bridge into Washington.

On television, Teresa Pringle saw a Renault on the bridge with its roof smashed down to the seats. It looked like Joe's car. Frantic, she called the television station, but they could not provide any more information. As time went on and Joe didn't come home, Teresa feared the worst.

The worst was confirmed late in the evening when police brought her Joe's wallet.

Ora Gray anxiously watched video of the Flight 90 crash scene on the evening news as it replayed over and over, paying close attention to a fleeting glimpse of one particular car on the 14th Street Bridge. A brown Mustang, its roof flattened, looked an awful lot like Mariella Spriggs's car. The daughter of a longtime friend, Spriggs had lived with Gray since her mother relocated to Boston for work three years earlier. Spriggs hadn't returned home from her job as a word processor in McLean.

The prospect was too painful to think about. Spriggs, twenty-seven years old, had just started a new job and was engaged to be married. The family had already suffered tragedy ten years earlier when her younger brother, Gerald, was killed in a car crash. There must have been hundreds of brown Mustangs in the area. What were the odds? Gray called friends and told them to turn on the news, asked them whether they recognized Spriggs's car.

An answer finally arrived at ten thirty that evening, when a DC police officer went to Gray's home and informed her that Spriggs had been killed on the 14th Street Bridge.

Washington police needed a place for families and friends to wait while Air Florida put together a list of passengers and survivors. The Twin Bridges Marriott was too close, within sight of debris and first responders searching for dead bodies. Police called Robert Perkins, manager of the Crystal City

Marriott, a newer hotel about a mile and a half away from the crash scene. Perkins volunteered the hotel's ballroom.

A year earlier, the same ballroom had been the venue for the reunion of families of fifty-three diplomats and citizens held hostage by Iranian revolutionaries since November 4, 1979. Hotelier J. Willard Marriott greeted the newly released hostages and treated them to free accommodations and a spread of crudités, cheese puffs, barbecued ribs, and an open bar. Twenty rooms were reserved for family members who wanted to stay the night at the hotel.

For the families of Flight 90 passengers, radio and television news stations cooperated by announcing that families should meet at the Crystal City Marriott. The hotel's switchboard was swamped with telephone calls from around the world, logging more than a thousand calls between 6:00 and 7:00 P.M.

The hotel set up thirty-five tables in the ballroom and laid out a spread of sandwiches, soup, rolls, and coffee. People began gathering in the ballroom almost as soon as they heard about the arrangements on the news. They arrived in groups and as couples. One woman had dropped off her fiancé, a biologist who was an authority on butterflies, at the airport. A man had put his elderly mother on the plane to Florida. They waited in the ballroom in silence, strangers bound by tragedy with little to talk about among themselves.

Press and cameras were kept outside of the ballroom to allow privacy. Media crowded the long corridor from the lobby to the ballroom, forcing distraught family members and friends to pass a gauntlet of reporters and television cameras.

Members of the clergy were allowed in the ballroom to provide comfort as people waited, including one fake priest who was recognized on news video as a con man from Ohio with an outstanding warrant. He was subsequently arrested.

Susan Bennett was among reporters outside the ballroom. She interviewed the Reverend Justin D. McClum, one of several clergy at the hotel. "It's been very quiet in there," he told her. "There's so much shock."

Bennett also interviewed David Frank, who was waiting to hear word about his fiancée, Nikki Felch. Her family had been trying to find out her fate. They heard that Flight 90 crash survivors were taken to National Hospital for Orthopaedics and Rehabilitation, but Nikki wasn't there.

Before returning to his mother and others who were waiting, Frank asked reporter Susan Bennett, "Do you want to come into the ballroom with me?"

Bennett thought about it. She could sneak in and get an exclusive, give readers a human-interest aspect of the story that nobody else had. But no. The families were entitled to their privacy.

"I can't do that," she told Frank. "That's too intrusive in a time of tragedy."

8:30 P.M.

The frenzy of activity in the fire department's dispatch center died down. Steve Souder pulled the cold hamburger from the paper bag that had been sitting on his desk all afternoon and evening. He put the burger in the micro-wave to warm up and took a bite. It was the first chance he'd had to eat all day. It was the best-tasting hamburger he'd ever had.

A nurse at MedStar Washington Hospital Center tracked down Frank with Felch's family at the Crystal City Marriott. Nikki was alive, although badly injured and suffering from exposure.

Frank burst into tears. "I thought she was dead," he said.

"They said she's suffering from exposure and some other injuries, but she's going to be okay," Frank told Bennett.

Tom Panther, who'd earlier driven past the crash scene in a taxicab, was sent to National Hospital to get the names of the survivors there.

Interviewing Olian, he asked where he was seated on the plane. "I wasn't on the plane," Olian told him. "I went in the water to help people."

Lenny Skutnik's main concern at National Hospital was money. He'd heard stories about how quickly medical bills can add up. "Is this going to cost me anything?" he asked a nurse before his hot shower.

Afterward, hospital staff brought him a chicken dinner. Afraid he was going to be charged for it, Skutnik declined the platter and asked for a cup of coffee.

A woman with a clipboard approached Skutnik and asked

for his Social Security number. Certain that he would end up owing money, Skutnik looked for an escape.

"Where's the bathroom," he asked her. Skutnik walked, as the woman indicated, and kept on walking through the lobby, where a stranger recognized him from television and gave him a ride home.

11:00 P.M.

During the evening, curious members of the public gathered along the Potomac and on the HOV bridge to look at the morbid scene.

Smokey Stover, the Arlington County Police chief, was lingering on the 14th Street Bridge when he encountered a woman standing at the railing, shivering. She had been driving on the bridge when the plane struck, and she saw everything. She saw bodies in the water and blood on the ice. The woman abandoned her car and didn't notice that it had been towed away. She had been standing there, in shock, for seven hours.

Gently guiding her to his cruiser, Stover gave the woman a ride to police headquarters so she could warm up and call somebody to take her home.

About eighty-five people gathered in the Crystal City Marriott ballroom. After five anxious hours of waiting, Robert Yarmy, Air Florida's regional director of sales, entered. The airline's ranking Washington executive, Yarmy was pressed into service to read an alphabetical list of the seventy-one passengers presumed dead and the names of the four passengers and one crew member who survived the crash and were being treated at area hospitals.

Grieving family members were confronted by a press scrum in the hotel corridor as they tried to leave the ballroom. News crews swiveled their cameras toward the door and turned on bright lights.

"Here come family members," one cameraman announced to his colleagues.

One couple exited the ballroom after having their worst fears confirmed. The life they had previously known was gone, and in its place was a deep void of pain.

The man had his arm around his inconsolably sobbing wife. A reporter thrust a microphone forward to capture the sound of the woman's raw grief. "Ah come on, give us a break for God's sake," her husband snapped.

Away from the Potomac River, the rest of Arlington County was quiet that night. While Arlington County Fire Department was on the scene of the Flight 90 crash, the county's 911 center received only one fire/EMS call. A woman went into labor and needed to get to the hospital. An ambulance crew handled that routine assignment.

The DC Fire Department didn't have it so easy. On the night of January 13, a fire that grew to three alarms tore through a half block of town houses at 1809–1815 19th Street NW.

For an unprecedented third time in twenty-four hours,

the fire department implemented Plan E to call in off-duty personnel. Fifteen engines, six trucks, and three rescue squads were dispatched to the 19th Street conflagration. More than 130 firefighters, including many who had been at the Potomac River for hours, worked through the night in subfreezing temperatures to control the fire.

Two firefighters, George Barksdale and Jim Reilly, were injured when a portion of a building collapsed and pinned them under debris.

11:30 P.M.

Flight 90 was the lead story on ABC News's *Nightline*. Ted Koppel interviewed Lenny Skutnik, who had been taken to the network's DC studio by limousine.

Koppel also spoke with Don Usher and Gene Windsor from the Eagle's Nest. Windsor, still wearing his bloody flight suit, was visibly uncomfortable appearing on live television and reluctant to talk.

The US Park Service kept the men at the Eagle's Nest to isolate them from the overwhelming media attention. Requests for interviews were coming in from around the world. Press trucks were parked outside their homes. The restricted access to the Eagle's Nest at least kept media at a distance.

Usher and Windsor wore their flight suits for the next three days, until family could bring them a fresh change of clothing.

part four
_____

Aftermath

On January 14, Washingtonians woke up to a chilly morning, with a temperature of twenty-one degrees Fahrenheit. The skies were overcast. A light snowfall gently dusted the city. The forecast called for an accumulation of four inches of snow through the day, turning to sleet or freezing rain by the evening.

For most people, it was just another Thursday. For some, it was the beginning of dramatically altered existences.

Dozens of families in Florida and the Washington area began planning memorial services for loved ones lost on Flight 90, on the 14th Street Bridge, and aboard train 410.

At 7:00 A.M., National Airport reopened for regularly scheduled flights. Schools in the Washington area were closed for a snow day. Most federal and District of Columbia offices closed so officials could deal with the aftermath of the previous day's catastrophes. Four Metrorail stations were closed to allow train 410 to be cut apart and shuttled out of the tunnel.

President Reagan surveyed the Flight 90 crash scene from Marine One on his way to Andrews Air Force Base en route to a speech in New York City. Later, First Lady Nancy Reagan would visit Priscilla Tirado at National Hospital.

Morning drive-time radio personality Howard Stern, the DC101 "shock jock" known for his outrageous and offensive antics, broadcast a gag in which he pretended to call the Air Florida reservations desk. "What's the price of a one-way ticket from National to the 14th Street Bridge?" he asked. "Is that going to be a regular stop?" Fired five months later — because he criticized the station management and not for his distasteful schtick — Stern moved to New York City, where he found fame and fortune.

Roger Olian went to the District of Columbia impound yard to retrieve his pickup truck. The impound fee was $50, almost all the money he had until payday. Olian placed damp bills on the counter and apologized for giving the clerk wet money. It was in my pocket when I went into the Potomac yesterday, he told the clerk.

"The airplane crash?" the clerk asked.

"Yeah," Olian said.

The clerk handed him the money back. "Keep it," he said.

When Olian went to turn the key in the ignition, the battery was dead. Fortunately, he had jumper cables in his truck.

From his bed at National Hospital, Joe Stiley called the *Washington Post* and television stations and held an impromptu press conference, much to the surprise and consternation of hospital staff.

"I knew we were too low and were going to hit something," he told reporters. "I think the pilot tried to abort but couldn't do it."

Stiley asked reporters whether they knew what had happened with his assistant, Nikki Felch. She wasn't with the others at the hospital. He thought she might have died. None of the press had any information about Felch. Stiley had no way of knowing that she had been flown to MedStar Washington Hospital Center.

Down the hall, with her family by her side, Priscilla Tirado was told about Jose and Jason. She cried quietly for days.

"I know they're at the bottom of the river," Tirado told a nurse. "It's so awful to think of them there. Is there any chance Jason might still be lying in Jose's arms?"

Navy divers resumed the grim task of recovering bodies and pieces of the airliner from the Potomac River. The Army Corps of Engineers built a temporary road capable of carrying heavy equipment from the George Washington Memorial Parkway along the riverside, and a 60-foot floating pontoon dock out onto the river. This infrastructure would also allow boats and wheeled vehicles to transport recovered bodies from the scene.

The Coast Guard tug *Capstan* stood guard over the scene from the water, accompanied by the fireboat, several police boats, and privately owned boats of curious onlookers. Police and firefighters in small inflatable craft broke up the ice with axes and picks.

When Flight 90 struck the water, the cockpit separated from the fuselage and the rest broke into three major pieces and numerous smaller fragments. None of the cabin floor remained intact. Every seat was extensively damaged, and most were torn away from the floor and pushed forward.

Debris was scattered over the area of a football field, extending from the northbound bridge, between the spans, and beneath the HOV bridge. Pieces of the right wing, which struck the P&P Construction truck crane, were found on the bridge deck.

Divers were divided into two teams, one to search for bodies and another to search for the flight data recorder and cockpit voice recorder. The divers' work was slow and tedious. Visibility in the murky river bottom was a foot or less. Grouped in teams of two or three, divers worked by touch, feeling around in the muck. Even with heated suits, divers couldn't work more than fifteen to twenty minutes at a time because of the extreme cold. Major parts of wreckage were marked with buoys and mapped. Officials then had to decide whether to lift the piece intact or recover the bodies first.

Bodies were lifted from the water, covered with a shroud, and brought by boat to the floating dock. From there, they were taken to a temporary morgue the DC medical examiner had set up in a tent. As much as possible, the recovery of bodies was done under tents and behind barriers to protect the deceased from the prying eyes of the public and media on the bridge. Bodies were given a preliminary examination at the scene. Inside the tent, each was tagged with a number. The medical examiner noted the decedent's height and weight, sex, estimated age, and physical characteristics such as hair and eye color. Watches, jewelry, and other personal property were laid out in the presence of police, photographed, and sealed in envelopes to return to families. After the field examination, bodies were taken to Washington for a full autopsy.

Among the passengers aboard Flight 90 were members of the Rapid Deployment Force returning to Fort MacDill in

The press lined up on the 14th Street Bridge to observe recovery activity on the Potomac River. Army Corps of Engineers

Tampa. One service member had classified documents in a valise chained to his wrist. The medical examiner contacted military officials to secure the material before the autopsy was conducted.

A construction crane was assembled on the 14th Street Bridge. Fragments of the airliner were lifted from the water and placed on a barge that had been brought in for that purpose or towed to shore, then transported to Hangar 6 at National Airport. Inside the hangar, pieces of the plane were reassembled and examined by NTSB investigators. The engines were taken to a Pratt & Whitney facility in Hartford, Connecticut, to be taken apart and inspected.

Seven more bodies were recovered on the second day, and then none at all for two days. Over the weekend divers began recovering a dozen or more bodies each day until the ninth day of searching. All the passengers and crew from Flight 90 were accounted for except for one, Priscilla Tirado's baby, Jason. Divers had systematically searched the entire area and were beginning to fear that Jason's body might not be found until the ice melted — or worse, may have been carried away by the current, never to be found.

On the seventh day of searching, Flight 90's flight data recorder and cockpit voice recorder were recovered. Both were in good condition and provided invaluable information for NTSB investigators.

On the tenth day, a diver searched beneath the floating dock and surfaced with a tiny body. "I got the baby!" he exclaimed.

A homicide detective, David Forbes, ran to the dock to take the body. He was supposed to put the baby in a body bag. But he couldn't. Jason was so small, just a tiny frozen thing. Forbes cradled Jason against his chest inside his jacket, covered the baby's face with his hand to shield him from news cameras, and walked him to the temporary morgue.

Postmortem examination of Flight 90 fatalities indicate that they did not have painful deaths. They did not have time to die of drowning or hypothermia. Most of the victims suffered devastating trauma of the head and chest that was instantly fatal. The remainder had lethal injuries that rapidly led to their demise before drowning or hypothermia could affect them.

The Jefferson Memorial provides a backdrop for navy divers searching the Potomac after the crash of Air Florida Flight 90. Army Corps of Engineers

Only one person endured the crash without any life-threatening injuries — Arland Williams. The cause of his death was determined to be drowning.

In an ironic twist, all of the survivors were seated in the smoking section in the rear of the plane. Smoking was banned on domestic flights of less than two hours in 1988. On Flight 90, the aft portion of the plane happened to be one of the places the fuselage split and separated. While the passengers up front suffered the full brunt of the collision with the bottom of the Potomac River, the tumbling of the tail section over vehicles on the 14th Street Bridge dissipated enough energy to make impact into the water survivable.

Underscoring the urgent need for better preparation for water incidents, the circumstances leading to the crash of Flight 90 nearly repeated ten days later.

On January 23, World Airways Flight 30 from Newark International Airport to Boston Logan International Airport landed on a slick runway during an ice storm. Unable to brake in time, the DC-10 slid off the end of the runway into the frozen Boston Harbor. The front portion of the plane, including the cockpit and forward galley, broke off from the fuselage and plunged the first row of passenger seats into thirty-degree water.

Initially, it was believed that all 210 passengers and the crew of twelve had survived the incident. However, it was discovered that two passengers were missing, seventy-year-old Walter Metcalf and his son Leo Metcalf, age forty. The Metcalfs had booked the flight at the last minute and were not listed on the manifest. They were among three people who fell into the water when the plane split open. Neither of them could swim. Their bodies were never recovered.

In Boston, as in Washington, rescue boats were icebound and could not immediately respond. Had the plane gone farther into Boston Harbor, passengers may have succumbed to hypothermia.

Both the crash of Flight 90 and the derailment of train 410 were the subject of investigations by the National Transportation Safety Board, as well as hearings in the US Senate and House of Representatives.

Two months after the crash, the NTSB held five days of public hearings at the Crystal City Marriott, in the same ballroom where families had held their vigil. Forty-six witnesses testified at the hearings, including four of the five survivors. After a seven-month investigation, the agency released its findings in a report.

The NTSB determined that the probable cause of Flight 90's crash was the failure of the pilots to use the engine anti-ice system, their decision to take off with snow and ice on airfoil surfaces of the plane, and Wheaton's failure to reject the takeoff during its early stage when Pettit noticed anomalous instrument readings.

The pilots' limited experience flying in winter conditions was cited by the NTSB as a contributing factor to the crash. Habituated as they were to flying in a warm climate, the importance of the engine anti-icing system was lost on Wheaton and Pettit as they worked through their checklist. Flying with snowy wings was a gamble that they lost. The Boeing 737 has a well-known tendency to pitch upward when the leading edge of a wing is contaminated with even traces of snow or ice. The correct response is to increase speed and pitch the plane downward, which the pilots of Flight 90 failed to do. The pilots should have pushed the throttle all the way, even at the risk of damaging the engines.

The NTSB also faulted deicing practices at National Airport. The investigation revealed several problems that resulted in deicing fluid that was much more dilute than it should have been being applied to aircraft. Guidelines suggest that given the weather conditions at the time, the deicing solution should have been at least 35 percent glycol and 65 percent water.

Deicing hose nozzles have a dial to select the concentration of the glycol/water mixture. At National Airport, the original nozzle provided by the equipment manufacturer had broken the previous November and was replaced with another nozzle that, unknown to the maintenance crew, didn't work the same. When the replacement nozzle was set to dispense a mixture of 35 percent glycol and 65 percent water, the concentration of glycol delivered was actually only 25 percent.

What's more, investigators discovered that the glycol in the airport storage tank was more dilute than expected. The tank should have contained 100 percent glycol, but lab testing revealed it was an 85 percent solution.

Tests by the FBI found that the glycol solution applied to Flight 90 was around 13 to 15 percent glycol, half the strength indicated for the weather conditions. The prolonged delay between deicing and takeoff allowed more snow to accumulate on the fuselage and wings.

Pettit noticed something wrong with the engine pressure ratio gauges when there was still time to safely reject the takeoff, as the NTSB learned from the cockpit voice recorder. Iinvestigators used electronic filters on the noise originating from the Pratt & Whitney jet engines during takeoff. By removing all other sources, they were able to isolate the whine produced by the engine's first-stage fan. They then compared the frequency of that sound with an identical Pratt & Whitney engine and were able to calculate the speed at which the first-stage fan was spinning.

The sound spectrum analysis revealed that the engines were producing 80 percent of the thrust needed for take-off. Pettit was right: The engine pressure ratio reading *was* wrong.

Underpowered and with lifting surfaces compromised by snow and ice, Flight 90 was doomed.

Flight 90 influenced a fundamental change in pilot training. One obvious question was why critical information wasn't acted upon. Should Pettit have been more assertive about what he noticed? Was it Wheaton's fault for not paying attention?

Pettit's inability to communicate the gravity of the problem he thought he saw, or Wheaton's inability to act on Pettit's input, is an issue that is not unique to an airliner cockpit. Working in any high-stakes arena, such as an operating room or the control room of a nuclear power station, depends upon effective communication and listening.

There may be any number of reasons why a team doesn't communicate effectively about critical safety issues, on either the speaking or the listening end — differences in rank, seniority, experience, or age. Many pilots, like Pettit and Wheaton, are former military personnel accustomed to strict adherence to a hierarchy and a deference to superior officers. The captain is in charge, and the captain is always right.

This problem of interpersonal communication led to the development of a new approach called Crew Resource Management (CRM). CRM is intended to reduce human error and create a culture of safety by encouraging situational awareness and effective communication.

CRM emerged from the 1978 crash of United Airlines Flight 173, a DC-8 inbound for Portland, Oregon, with 181 passengers and a crew of eight aboard. On approach to the airport, an indicator in the cockpit showed that the nose gear was not down. The captain flew a holding pattern while they worked to troubleshoot the problem.

Flight 173 circled over the suburbs of Portland for more than an hour. The crew was so concentrated on the problematic nose gear that nobody kept an eye on the fuel gauge. The plane ran out of fuel and crashed in a residential neighborhood, killing ten people and injuring twenty-three.

CRM was introduced by United Airlines in 1981. Its adoption in commercial aviation accelerated after the crash of Flight 90. CRM has been adapted for other high-risk areas such as aerospace, the maritime industry, construction, firefighting, and medicine.

Had CRM been in use before Flight 90, Pettit may have disregarded Wheaton's seniority when he realized something was wrong and either rejected the takeoff or pushed the thrust to the firewall to avoid catastrophe.

Flight 90 was one of the most consequential aviation disasters in modern history. The NTSB made twenty-one recommendations to the FAA in the report of their investigation, most of which have since been adopted. Every person who travels on a commercial airline today benefits from critical safety improvements adopted largely because of Flight 90.

Flight 90 focused attention on the hazards of ice and snow on wing surfaces. Before the crash, deicing was left to the discretion of pilots. The FAA developed new rules about deicing and required enhanced training for ground crews and pilots. The concentration of glycol in deicing fluid was increased, and it must now be applied according to specifications. The FAA established a time limit between deicing and takeoff, and requires a plane to be deiced again if it exceeds this limit.

As Wheaton and Pettit suggested in jest, many major airports have installed deicing facilities near runways so glycol solution can be applied just before takeoff.

Flotation vests for commercial aviation were redesigned for the first time since World War II. The modern flotation vest is easier to put on and fastens with one simple buckled strap. The inflatable compartments are designed to keep a person upright with their head out of the water without any effort, even if a victim is unconscious.

By remaining upright, survivors can huddle together to conserve heat and increase their chance of survival, unlike a group of people paddling while clutching floatable seat cushions. The modern personal flotation device is an improvement even if there aren't enough to go around. One vest provides enough buoyancy for two or more people.

The FAA now requires passengers to receive preflight instruction about flotation vests on all flights, whether over open water or not.

Today the FAA requires major airports to have emergency plans to rescue victims of an aircraft accident from significant bodies of water or marshland adjacent to the airport or beneath the departure or approach flight paths of commercial air carriers.

Every person who flies today benefits because people died on January 13, 1982. The 150 passengers and five crew aboard US Airways Flight 1549 were better prepared for a water landing in 2009 when the Airbus A320 struck a flock of birds and lost engine power shortly after takeoff from LaGuardia Airport. Pilot Chesley "Sully" Sullenberger ditched the plane in the Hudson River. Everybody survived.

The crash of Flight 90 was the beginning of the end for Air Florida. Photos of the airliner's severed tail section lifted by crane from the icy Potomac River were plastered on the front pages of newspapers across the country. Reservations ground to a halt.

Air Florida paid $50 million to survivors of the crash and relatives of those who were killed. Details about the distribution of the funds were kept confidential except for a few cases. Among the exceptions is Priscilla Tirado, who received $3.25 million for her loss.

US airlines sustained catastrophic economic losses in 1982. Air Florida struggled for another two and a half years before declaring bankruptcy and ceasing operations in July 1984.

The derailment of train 410 was the subject of three investigations. Aside from the NTSB and WMATA's internal investigation, an independent panel cosponsored by the American Public Transportation Association conducted a third investigation.

The NTSB conducted a nine-month investigation of the Metrorail derailment and issued a final report in October 1982. The agency faulted Metrorail's OCC for allowing trains to use the interlocking without correcting the problem with the A-1 rail switch that caused the derailment. The OCC had failed to order repairs to the switch for three successive days leading up to the incident.

The investigation report laid blame on the on-scene supervisor for his failure to check the switch and rails before reversing the train and on the train operator for not recognizing the derailment and applying the brakes in a timely manner.

The cause of the Metro derailment was attributed to a malfunctioning switch and the failure of several WMATA employees to follow accepted practices. The NTSB also faulted the WMATA's management and emergency procedures.

Two Metrorail employees were disciplined for their role in the derailment of train 410. Supervisor James E. Davis was suspended for ninety working days with no pay, and train operator Michael Greene was suspended for sixty working days with no pay. In addition, both men were prohibited from working any job involving train operations in the future.

The WMATA's internal investigation also faulted supervisory controller Kenneth Banks and assistant supervisor Paul Hobgood Jr. but did not recommend any disciplinary action against either man. The panel recommended several improvements, including handheld two-way radios for train operators that are independent of the train's electrical supply, better signage to indicate power lines and exits in rail tunnels, the acquisition of emergency equipment for Metro stations, and the development of emergency response teams.

The WMATA enhanced its radio system, placing repeaters in underground stations and tunnels so police and fire personnel can communicate without disruption.

The agency posted instructions for emergency escape in Metro cars, labeled the lever to manually open the doors in an emergency, and installed pop-out emergency windows in railcars.

To avoid a repeat of the confusion over who is in charge of the OCC, the WMATA implemented a new policy that designates a supervisor to take command during an emergency.

The WMATA's most critical error was a failure of imagination, the inability to envision the circumstances that led to tragedy. Critics warned that Metrorail was headed for disaster unless more attention was paid to safety and emergency planning. Agency officials placed unwarranted confidence in the perfection of its automated systems and touted the subway as the safest in the world.

The WMATA "always had an 'it-will-never-happen-here' attitude," said NTSB staff member William Gossard, who has studied rail and tunnel accidents. "They have always been somewhat arrogant."

Metrorail's safety record has been less than ideal, with numerous serious incidents since then:

January 6, 1996: A Metrorail operator was killed when the computer-controlled braking failed, allowing a train to overrun the platform at Shady Grove station, striking an unoccupied train.

November 3, 2004: An out-of-service Red Line train rolled backward into a train at the Woodley Park station, injuring twenty riders. Had the train at the platform been full, according to accident investigators, scores of passengers would have been killed.

June 22, 2009: A Red Line train collided with another train that stopped short of the platform at the Fort Totten station, killing nine riders and injuring seventy others. As with the January 13, 1982, derailment, the injured and dead were trapped for hours until rescuers cut away twisted metal.

November 29, 2009: Two out-of-service trains collided at the Falls Church rail yards, injuring three Metrorail workers.

October 7, 2019: Two out-of-service trains collided in the tunnel between the Foggy Bottom and Farragut West stations, injuring two operators.

The chaotic disorder and lack of coordination on January 13 are not uncommon in large-scale incidents, particularly those involving multiple agencies or jurisdictions that are unaccustomed to working together. To avoid these problems, emergency services developed an organizational approach called the Incident Command System (ICS).

The ICS emerged after the catastrophic 1970 wildfire season in Southern California. In a thirteen-day period, almost eight hundred wildfires burned nearly six hundred thousand acres, destroying more than seven hundred buildings and causing the deaths of sixteen people. Firefighters from throughout Southern California were dispatched to simultaneous fires over far-flung areas. Fire departments established multiple command posts and fire camps, with little coordination among them. The response was so chaotic that fire vehicles often passed each other going in opposite directions.

The ICS is a standardized on-scene incident management system, an off-the-shelf organizational structure that can be adapted to any kind of incident. The system is a set of common ground rules that establish a command structure, lines of communication, and clear delineation of responsibilities.

Since its development in the 1970s among fire services, the ICS has been adopted by the Federal Emergency Management Agency (FEMA) and emergency services throughout the country.

The larger problem of the overall disorganization, inter-jurisdictional squabbles, and lack of effective command that reigned on January 13 was addressed by the Metropolitan Washington Council of Governments. In the weeks following, COG conducted a survey of emergency preparedness in the District of Columbia, Montgomery and Prince George's

Counties in Maryland, and five city and county jurisdictions in Virginia. Some plans were more robust than others, but overall, the state of preparedness was woefully inadequate to manage a response to the type of incident that had just occurred.

The COG survey found that information in written disaster plans was infrequently, if ever, updated. Some plans were years old, gathering dust in filing cabinets. They were drawn up without the participation and input of neighboring jurisdictions. Plans were never tested in real-life scenarios, never developed beyond bullet-pointed ideas.

Existing disaster plans looked good printed with a cover page and bound in a ring binder but proved hollow when it mattered. Of all the disaster plans in all the agencies in the eight cities and counties surveyed by COG, not one of them identified Metrorail as a potential hazard. With a couple of exceptions, the plans did not consider the possibility of a Metro accident. None of the plans included provisions for what to do in the event of a disaster that affects multiple jurisdictions. None of the plans regarded the possibility of multiple incidents occurring at once.

Every agency in the COG survey reported that they reviewed, revised, and updated their emergency preparedness plans in light of the events of January 13.

In February 1982, COG assembled a task force consisting of fire and police chiefs from Washington and adjacent jurisdictions, along with representatives from other emergency response agencies. The task force formed twenty committees to focus on specific areas such as communications and training. Much of the business of the task force was related to jurisdictional issues, mutual aid, and command authority at incident scenes — all areas that were problems on January 13.

Within six months, the task force issued its report with dozens of recommended improvements, ranging from closing radio frequency gaps to advanced training for first responders. COG's report even included a timetable and objective milestones to assess progress.

This report wasn't bound and shelved with the others. What made it different was that the mayors and elected officials in Washington and the adjacent counties and municipalities bought into the process. Straightening out the region's disaster response was a directive from the top down. The recent trauma of January 13 made it imperative.

The region conducted its first large-scale multi-jurisdiction mock disaster exercise in November 1982, with the Washington and Arlington County fire departments and rescue squads and numerous police and emergency agencies. More than twelve hundred people participated in the drill, which was designed as a worst-case scenario to test the system. The simulation involved a derailment and fire between Metrorail stations in a tunnel beneath the Potomac River, with a loss of third-rail power. More than two hundred volunteer "victims" were transported by ambulance and helicopter to ten area hospitals.

The exercise was considered a success, with command, communications, and coordination dramatically improved over January 13. The WMATA tested the fire department radio repeater system in the tunnel, a new fire/rescue phone system, and a prototype evacuation cart that travels on the rails.

The lessons learned from January 13 have reverberated over the years since. The response to the attack on the Pentagon on 9/11 benefited from the use of the Incident Command System and interoperability — the ability of fire and police personnel to communicate with each other by radio. Emergency services across the country are increasingly interoperable and follow ICS principles.

The park police replaced Eagle One with an updated Bell helicopter equipped for rescue, with a hoist and a basket litter. The hoist has proved valuable on medevac flights and lifesaving when Eagle One evacuated personnel during an active shooter situation at the Navy Yard on September 16, 2013.

After a second career with the US Department of Interior, the former Eagle One was restored and painted its original park police colors and now hangs in the National Law Enforcement Museum in Washington, DC.

National Airport acquired a second water rescue craft — another airboat — and constructed a second boat ramp at the northern end of the airport. In 1998, the airport was renamed Ronald Reagan Washington National Airport.

The District of Columbia implemented a centralized dispatch center for police, fire, and EMS to eliminate cross-agency communication problems.

All of the survivors of Flight 90 suffered long-term physical and psychological effects from their experience, including signs of post-traumatic stress disorder: anxiety, sleeplessness, and flashbacks. Many sought therapy to help recover.

Nikki Felch didn't have sensation in her hands for six months. She developed a severe infection in a wound on her foot, acquired in the Potomac, that required repeated hospitalization and surgical procedures. Felch spent most of a year in the hospital and nearly lost her foot.

Felch married David Frank in May 1982. She needed a cane, wrapped in lace matching her bridal gown, to walk down the aisle. She flew again in August, seven months after Flight 90, with her husband by her side. Although terrified, she felt that air travel was necessary to get on with her life.

Ultimately, Felch divorced and moved to Florida, where she volunteered with an organization supporting children with HIV. She returned to the Washington area and died of pancreatic cancer in 2002 at forty-nine years of age.

January 13 divided Joe Stiley's life into before and after. Nothing was the same again. After being discharged from the hospital, Stiley moved in with his parents in Idaho for a long recuperation. He underwent eighteen months of grueling physical therapy to be able to walk again.

When Stiley eventually returned to GTE, he found that somebody had been hired to fill his position. He had nothing to do at work, and still had difficulty walking. People stared at him, some badge of notoriety that he'd never asked for and didn't want. He was that guy from Flight 90. He left GTE after two weeks.

Stiley's brush with death forced him to reconsider his

Joe Stiley, Nikki Felch, Roger Olian, and Bert Hamilton in November 1982. David Hume Kennerly/Getty

life, his goals and priorities. The conclusion his reflection brought him included a divorce and moving to the Pacific Northwest, where he ran computer-related businesses for many years.

In his later years, Stiley moved to Puerto Escondido, a resort town on the Pacific coast of Mexico, and bought a bed-and-breakfast. He lives in a subtropical paradise and vows never to be cold again.

Within months of the Flight 90 crash, Bert Hamilton left his job at Fairchild Industries and had to apply for disability benefits because of his injuries. He often gave talks to civic groups and service organizations about how his near-death experience forced him to reevaluate his life. "I believe God had a reason for sparing my life," Hamilton told a reporter. He died of natural causes in 2003.

After five months of recuperation, Kelly Duncan returned to work as a flight attendant for Air Florida. As with Hamilton, her experience on January 13 rekindled her religious faith. Duncan left the airline in 1984 to teach in a Christian preschool. She married professional tennis player John Moore and is mother to three children. Kelly Moore is now retired in Florida.

Priscilla Tirado never fully recovered from the loss of her husband and child. On the first anniversary of the crash, she was arrested for driving under the influence. Tirado rarely speaks with reporters and was not interviewed for this book. In 1987, she told a reporter, "It's still hard for me. Sometimes I have my days. I had a good life with Jose. He was real good to me."

Tirado never remarried. She lives in Florida and works with rescue animals.

Arland Williams became a symbol of selflessness and altruism, the man in the water who handed a lifeline to others. The 14th Street Bridge span struck by Flight 90 was rededicated as the Arland Williams Bridge.

Those who were involved in the rescue of Flight 90 survivors received numerous awards and accolades.

Don Usher and Gene Windsor were given an award for valor from the US Department of the Interior. At the cere-

Flight attendant Kelly Duncan with pilot Don Usher and rescue technician Gene Windsor in November 1982. David Hume Kennerly/Getty

mony in their honor with Secretary James Watt, Usher was characteristically modest. "They call us heroes, but I don't know about that," he said to a reporter. "We just did what we were supposed to do."

John Leck was given a commendation from the DC Fire Department for assisting in the rescue of Priscilla Tirado.

Don Usher, Gene Windsor, Lenny Skutnik, and Roger Olian were honored by the Carnegie Hero Fund Commission, a private organization that awards the Carnegie Medal to "individuals who risk death or serious injury to an extraordinary degree saving or attempting to save the lives of others." The Carnegie Medal is North America's highest civilian honor for heroism and comes with a $3,000 cash award. Olian donated half of his award to the National Hospital for Orthopaedics and Rehabilitation.

Chester Panzer left WJLA for Washington's NBC affiliate, WRC, where he has been ever since, now in semi-retirement. His breathtaking video of the Flight 90 rescue was nominated for a Pulitzer Prize in the category of news photography, because stills of the video were printed in newspapers around the world. But his work was ruled ineligible because the Pulitzer is not awarded for video. Panzer did receive a local Emmy from the Washington, DC, chapter of the National Academy of Television Arts and Sciences for spot news coverage. He continues to work part-time in videography in the Washington area and lives in Northern Virginia.

Dave Statter was hired by WTOP and remained at the station as news and traffic reporter until 1985, when he joined WUSA-TV as a general assignment reporter. Since 2007 he has edited STATter911.com, which covers fire and EMS.

Lenny Skutnik became an instant celebrity as an American hero. A businessman offered to pay his rent for two years. Mississippi governor William F. Winter dispatched his plane to transport native-born Skutnik and his wife, Linda, to Jacksonville for a private dinner and a visit with family in Macomb, Mississippi. Rolex gave Skutnik a Submariner wristwatch to replace the Timex he lost in the snow on the Potomac riverbank. Air Florida gave Skutnik a lifetime pass for him and his family.

Less than two weeks after the crash of Flight 90, President Ronald Reagan invited Skutnik to the State of the Union

Address. Reagan paid tribute to Skutnik, who received a standing ovation at the joint session of Congress. Skutnik's appearance began the tradition of honoring an invited guest in the gallery during the State of the Union that has been followed ever since.

Overnight, Skutnik was in demand for interviews for broadcast and in print. For a while he was accommodating to the press, welcoming them into his home. The press took advantage of his generosity, racking up long-distance charges on his phone. Skutnik rarely talks to reporters anymore and declined to be interviewed for this book.

In 2007, Skutnik talked about that day with a *Washington Post* reporter. "I wasn't a hero," he said. "I was just someone who helped another human being. We're surrounded by heroes. What made this different is that it was caught on video and went all over the world."

Skutnik retired from the Congressional Budget Office in 2010 and lives in Pennsylvania.

Air Florida asked Roger Olian if the airline could do anything for him to show its gratitude. He told the airline that they didn't owe him anything. He did what he did that day because he had to. Once he was aware of people in peril, "I couldn't turn my back on them," he said.

Months after the crash, Joe Stiley, Bert Hamilton, and Kelly Duncan visited Olian at the sheet metal shop at St. Elizabeths Hospital. Stiley told Olian that he heard his words of encouragement and saw him claw through the ice. His action was not futile. It helped them survive, Stiley told him, and gave them hope in a hopeless situation.

"So often in life we are disappointed in ourselves," Olian told a reporter. "We let ourselves down for not doing the right thing, or being the right person, or being as good as we should be. This is one time in my life when I can look back and say to myself that I did my best, the best I could ever do."

Olian worked at St. Elizabeths Hospital until staff reductions forced him into early retirement in 2002. For several years, he ran a tree-trimming service in Northern Virginia. Now he and his wife live in Pennsylvania.

Don Usher continued to fly for the park police while attending law school at the University of Baltimore. He received his law degree in 1987 and two years later left the park police aviation unit for a position in the legal division of the Federal Law Enforcement Training Center in Brunswick, Georgia.

Usher's career as a pilot was mostly over, except for a part-time gig with the local mosquito control authority flying a small, two-seater Hughes 269 helicopter on low-level runs a few feet off the ground, spraying insecticide over the crepuscular lowlands of Glynn County. He is now retired.

Gene Windsor remained a rescue technician in the park police aviation unit until his retirement in 1993. He then moved to South Carolina, where he worked as a police officer for several years. Windsor died of a brain aneurysm in 2014 at age seventy-four.

There were countless others who were involved in the events of January 13 in ways big and small. Their names will never be known. Whether stepping into icy water, pulling over to let an emergency vehicle get by, relaying a message, assisting a stranger to walk out of a subway tunnel — each of these acts mattered, and each contributed to help people survive.

IN MEMORIAM

Flight 90 Fatalities

Gordon Ray Anderson
Jo Ann Blake
David Wesley Boer
Jane R. Burka
Kathleen Frances Burke
John Gordon Calvin
Joseph L. Carluccio
Major Errol David Champagne
Colonel Edward Roger Cobb
Sophie Davis
Cathleen Lynn Del Monte
Sergeant Major James B. Dixon
Rex Allen Ellis
James L. Erickson
Robert L. Essary
James Ronald Fako
Thomas Fisher
Judith Rosalind Foer
Susan Mae Fusco
Michael C. Garland
Donald Perkins Gilmore Jr.
George Graham
Elizabeth Hanson
Herman Haven
Major Ralph Herman

Lieutenant Colonel Herbert Leo Hiller
James Columbus Hobbs
Edward James Horton
Arnold Ivener
Eric R. Kauffman
Terrence Klasky
Christine Mary Krzanowski
David Edward Krzanowski
Dr. Edward Francis Michael Krzanowski
Karen Ann Krzanowski
Robert Joseph Laudani
Michael David Lauderdale
Benson Levinson
Dr. William D. Little Jr.
Lieutenant Colonel George G. Mattar
Chalmers Moore Stirling McIlwaine Jr.
Gertie Lee McNeely
Lee McNeely
Richard O. Miller
Harriet Murek
Leon Murek
S. Pibbs
T. Pibbs
Barbara Ann Piontek
Brian Thomas Piontek
Mary Theresa Piontek
Francis Pipes
Marion Player
Dr. Robert Parker Shubinski

IN MEMORIAM

Robert Elliot Silberglied
William Butler Skiles
Theodore Henry Smolen
Eugene Soune
Dorothy B. Stemper
Walter Sutton
Howard Kenneth Testerman
Jason Manuel Tirado
Jose Tirado-Del-Moral
Robert Vernon Trexler
John Thomas Ventura
Arthur John Viehman Jr.
Celeste B. Weingarten
Arlen Dean Williams Jr.
Sharon Elizabeth Wood
Stanley D. Woodard
William Zondler

Crew Fatalities

Donna Charleene Adams
Marilyn Nichols
Roger Allan Pettit
Larry Michael Wheaton

14th Street Bridge Fatalities

Ray Bowles
Joe Nathan Pringle

IN MEMORIAM

Michael Saunders
Marilla Spriggs

Metrorail Fatalities

Mariano Cortez
Mary L. O'Meara
Mildred M. Morgan

AUTHOR'S NOTE

I'm grateful for the cooperation of those who shared their recollections of January 13, 1982, including Vincent Ambers, Tim Anderson, Susan Bennett, John Brazier, Kevin Byrne, Joe Dean, Craig DeAtley, Aldo De La Cruz, Steven Felch, Thomas Hoffman, Steven Holl, Tim Jones, John Leck, Kenneth Madden, Dave Mastric, Roger Olian, Tom Overman, Tom Panther, Chester Panzer, Howard Piansky, Reed Pullan, James Schneider, Don Scott Jr., Paul Shaw, Richard Singer, Ed Smith, Steven Souder, Joe Stiley, Ruby Mae Thomas, Anthony Tisdale, Don Usher, and Cindi Ziegler.

I owe debts of gratitude for the assistance of former DC firefighter James Embry, Rich Dzierwa of *Firehouse* magazine, Tom Canavan of the National Law Enforcement Museum, Tre Moreland of the WMATA transit police, Jared Galloway of the National Naval Aviation Museum, David Goldfarb, Dave Statter, and Nick Thomas.

Most of all, I am thankful for my wife and children. This book would not be possible without their love, support, and patience.

SOURCES

The following sources appear in an order that corresponds
to the narrative flow of *The Worst Day*.

PART ONE

"Vacant Upshur health clinic destroyed by predawn fire." *Washington Post*,
January 13, 1982.

"Emergency Preparedness in the Washington Metropolitan Area." Hearings
before the House Committee on the District of Columbia, 97th Congress,
p 4 (1982). Testimony of Donald Devine and Patrick S. Korten, Office of
Personnel Management.

"Emergency Preparedness in the Washington Metropolitan Area." Hearings
before the House Committee on the District of Columbia, 97th Congress,
p 77 (1982). Testimony of Thomas Downs, District of Columbia Transportation Department.

"Emergency Preparedness in the Washington Metropolitan Area." Hearings
before the House Committee on the District of Columbia, 97th Congress,
p 42 (1982). Testimony of Richard W. Page and Lawrence M. Engleman,
Washington Metropolitan Area Transit Administration.

"Emergency Preparedness in the Washington Metropolitan Area." Hearings
before the Senate Subcommittee on Government Efficiency and the
District of Columbia, 98th Congress, p 304 (1982). Testimony of Patrick S.
Korten, Office of Personnel Management.

Eppinger, Josh. "The most amazing rescue of '82." *Popular Mechanics*, January
1983.

McAden, Fitz. "Flight 90 shook, limped skyward." *Miami Herald*, March 2,
1982.

"It felt like it was going to shake to pieces." *Bradenton Herald*, March 2, 1982.

McMahon, Patrick. "Flight 90 'felt like it was going to shake to pieces.'"
Tampa Bay Times, March 2, 1982.

Newman, Bud. "Air Florida survivors relive terror of crash." *Palm Beach Post*,
March 2, 1982.

Orrick, Bentley. "Flight 90 – It began as any other flight . . ." *Tampa Tribune*,
January 17, 1982.

McAden, Fritz. "Flight 90 shook violently, crashed." *Miami Herald*, March 2, 1982.

"Life and death of Air Florida Flight 90." *Miami Herald*, January 17, 1982.

Van Dyne, Larry; Pekkanen, John; Rapoport, Daniel. "A false sense of security." *Washingtonian*, October 1982.

Adams, Rich. "DC disaster crisis." *Firehouse*, March 1982.

Battiata, Mary. "Too late to join friends, man sat at rear of plane – and lived." *Washington Post*, January 14, 1982.

Yoffe, Emily. "Afterward." *New York Times Magazine*, August 4, 2002.

"A horrible impact – then icy death." *Chicago Tribune*, January 10, 1983.

"Survivors of crash remember little more than numbing cold." *Daily Advance*, January 15, 1982.

PART TWO

United States. National Transportation Safety Board. (1982). Aircraft Accident Report: Air Florida, Inc. Boeing 737-222, N62AF, Collision with 14th Street Bridge, near Washington National Airport, Washington, DC, January 13, 1982. Report No. NTSB-AAR-82-8. Retrieved from https://www.ntsb.gov/investigations/AccidentReports/Reports/AAR8208.pdf. Accessed February 22, 2025.

"Emergency Preparedness in the Washington Metropolitan Area." Hearings before the House Committee on the District of Columbia, 97th Congress, p 757 (1982). Testimony of James Wilding, Washington Metropolitan Airports.

"Emergency Preparedness in the Washington Metropolitan Area." Hearings before the House Committee on the District of Columbia, 97th Congress, p 777 (1982). Testimony of Theodore P. Judd and Joseph M. Schwind, Air Line Pilots Association.

"Emergency Preparedness in the Washington Metropolitan Area." Hearings before the House Committee on the District of Columbia, 97th Congress, p 359 (1982). Air Line Pilots Association presentation.

"Emergency Preparedness in the Washington Metropolitan Area." Hearings before the House Committee on the District of Columbia, 97th Congress, p 390 (1982). National Transportation Safety Board Bureau of Technology February 8, 1982, Human Factors Group Factual Report.

Lewthwaite, Gilbert A. "D.C. airport mixes danger, safety." *Baltimore Sun*, January 14, 1982.

SOURCES

"Despite safety concerns, airport likely to survive." *Miami Herald*, January 17, 1982.

"Crash is 2nd in National Airport's 42-year history." *Orlando Sentinel*, January 14, 1982.

Bedwell, Don. "First in-state airline begins flights today." *Miami Herald*, September 27, 1972.

Johnson, Robert. "Airline zoomed after 7 lean years." *Orlando Sentinel*, January 14, 1982.

"Flight 90 called a 'hot route.'" *Orlando Sentinel*, January 14, 1982.

McQueen, Mike. "Air Florida's story was one success." *Wilmington Morning News*, January 14, 1982.

"Deregulation leads to younger, less experienced pilots." *Chicago Tribune*, January 9, 1983.

"Flight 90's de-icing solution weaker than setting showed." *Bradenton Herald*, March 4, 1982.

Newman, Bud. "Crew chief pepped up de-icing dose after crash." *Miami News*, March 4, 1982.

"An airplane waits in the snow for a date with disaster." *Chicago Tribune*, January 9, 1983.

McMahon, Patrick. "Air Florida pilots got cold weather warning." *Tampa Bay Times*, March 2, 1982.

McAden, Fitz. "Fatal Flight 90 pilot was 'one of a very few' to fail examinations." *Miami Herald*, Julu 10, 1982.

"'The lousiest airport in the world.'" *Syracuse Post-Standard*, January 14, 1982.

Bender, Judith. "A crash long feared at a close-in airport." *Newsday*, January 14, 1982.

"De-icing plane similar to de-icing auto windshield." *Tampa Tribune*, January 15, 1982.

"De-icer was weaker than thought." *Miami Herald*, March 4, 1982.

"Here are probers' findings so far." *Miami Herald*, January 17, 1982.

"Ice is focus of crash probe." *Miami Herald*, January 16, 1982.

"Tests: De-icer was at half strength." *Fort Lauderdale News*, March 4, 1982.

Koza, Patricia. "The air traffic controller who handled the final seconds of Flight 90." *United Press International*, March 2, 1982.

Air Florida PT2 Probe Animation. Federal Aviation Administration, January 7, 2021. https://youtu.be/m6rqMnmxikU. Accessed February 24, 2025.

Air Florida Takeoff Animation. Federal Aviation Administration, January 7, 2021. https://youtu.be/qZsT7jeNpe8. Accessed February 24, 2025.

"Bowling Green man on bridge when plane hit." *Freemont News Messenger*, January 14, 1982.

Smith, Mike "SC native on bridge during crash." *Sumter Daily Item*, January 18, 1982.

PART THREE

United States. National Transportation Safety Board. (1982). Railroad Accident Report: Derailment of Washington Metropolitan Area Transit Authority Train No, 10 at Smithsonian Interlocking, January 13, 1982. Report No. NTSB-RAR-82-6. Retrieved from https://www.ntsb.gov/investigations/AccidentReports/Reports/RAR8206.pdf. Accessed February 22, 2025.

"Emergency Preparedness in the Washington Metropolitan Area." Hearings before the House Committee on the District of Columbia, 97th Congress, p 76 (1982). Testimony of Norman Richardson and Maurice D. Kilby, District of Columbia Fire Department.

"Emergency Preparedness in the Washington Metropolitan Area." Hearings before the House Committee on the District of Columbia, 97th Congress, p 74 (1982). Testimony of Maurice D. Kilby, McEldon L. Fleming, and Rayfield Alfred, District of Columbia Fire Department.

"Emergency Preparedness in the Washington Metropolitan Area." Hearings before the House Committee on the District of Columbia, 97th Congress, p 74 (1982). Testimony of Maurice Turner and William Anastos, District of Columbia Metropolitan Police Department.

"Emergency Preparedness in the Washington Metropolitan Area." Hearings before the House Committee on the District of Columbia, 97th Congress, p 1803 (1982). Testimony of Davis S. Dwyer and J. S. Vayer, Bethesda Chevy Chase Fire Department.

"Emergency Preparedness in the Washington Metropolitan Area." Hearings before the House Committee on the District of Columbia, 97th Congress, p 381 (1982). Bethesda Chevy Chase Rescue Squad J. S. Vayer letter dated March 17, 1982.

"Emergency Preparedness in the Washington Metropolitan Area." Hearings before the House Committee on the District of Columbia, 97th Congress, p 74 (1982). Testimony of Norman Richardson and Maurice D. Kilby, District of Columbia Fire Department.

"Emergency Preparedness in the Washington Metropolitan Area." Hearings before the House Committee on the District of Columbia, 97th Congress, p 20 (1982). Testimony of Gale Braden, Patricia Goldman, and Francis McAdams, National Transportation Safety Board.

"Emergency Preparedness in the Washington Metropolitan Area." Hearings before the House Committee on the District of Columbia, 97th Congress, p 324 (1982). District of Columbia Fire Department chronology of events surrounding both incidents.

"Emergency Preparedness in the Washington Metropolitan Area." Hearings before the Senate Subcommittee on Government Efficiency and the District of Columbia, 98th Congress, p 108 (1982). Testimony of Mark Smith, MD, division of emergency medicine, George Washington University, and Frank L. Brown, MD, director of emergency medicine, Washington Hospital Center.

"Emergency Preparedness in the Washington Metropolitan Area." Hearings before the Senate Subcommittee on Government Efficiency and the District of Columbia, 98th Congress, p 304 (1982). Testimony of Patrick S. Korten, Office of Personnel Management.

"Emergency Preparedness in the Washington Metropolitan Area." Hearings before the Senate Subcommittee on Government Efficiency and the District of Columbia, 98th Congress, p 66. Report of the Metropolitan Emergency Response Task Force, Metropolitan Washington Council of Governments.

Page, Susan; Lane, Earl; Waldman Myron S. "74 die as jet crashes into DC bridge." *Newsday*, January 14, 1982.

Greve, Frank. "Survivors cling to wreckage." *Orlando Sentinel*, January 14, 1982.

"81 dead in Air Florida crash; divers chop at ice on Potomac." *Miami Herald*, January 14, 1982

"'Helpless' diver saves her." *Orlando Sentinel*, January 14, 1982.

Montgomery, Dave. "Men resort to heroism in tragedy." *Fort Worth Star-Telegram*, January 14, 1982.

Newman, Bud; Katz, Barbara; McCarthy, Kathy. "'The plane started to shake and the next thing I knew I was in the water.'" *Miami News*, January 14, 1982.

Perl, Peter. "A fatal day." *Washington Post*, January 21, 1982.

"Plane smashes cars, plunges into icy river; 81 are believed killed." *Des Moines Register*, January 14, 1982.

"Jet hits packed DC bridge; snow paralyzes traffic here." *Baltimore Sun*, January 14, 1982.

Montes, Sue Anne Pressley. "In a moment of horror, rousing acts of courage." *Washington Post*, January 13, 2007.

Yengich, Nick. "'That man earned a place in heaven.'" *Baltimore Evening Sun,* January 14, 1982.

Koza, Patricia. "'USAir 172, would you do me a favor?'" *United Press International,* January 30, 1982.

Cullen, Robert B. "Witnesses say airliner 'too low.'" *Messenger-Inquirer,* January 14, 1982

"Story of REACT involvement in DC airplane crash." *The REACTor,* March-April, 1982.

O'Leary, Dennis S. (1982). "Managing a hospital under crisis." In R. Adams Cowley (Ed.), *Proceedings: First International Assembly on Emergency Medical Services,* Baltimore MD, June 13–17, 1982.

Esch, Victor H. (1982). "Air crash on the Potomac: Onsite problems." In R. Adams Cowley (Ed.), *Proceedings: First International Assembly on Emergency Medical Services,* Baltimore MD, June 13–17, 1982.

Edelstein, Sol (1982). "Metro subway accident." In R. Adams Cowley (Ed.), *Proceedings: First International Assembly on Emergency Medical Services,* Baltimore MD, June 13–17, 1982.

Sanders, Jacquin; Keefer, Beirne. "Palm 90: 2 hours of life – and a minute of death." *Tampa Bay Times,* January 8, 1984.

Shaffer, Ron; Perl, Peter. "Series of disasters paralyzes capital area at rush hour." *Washington Post,* January 14, 1982.

Deitz, Ed. "Faces of tragedy." *Tampa Tribune,* January 15, 1982.

"53 aboard jet listed Tampa as destination." *Orlando Sentinel,* January 14, 1982.

Sanders, Jacquin; Keefer, Beirne. "Palm 90 survivors: Silence, terror, and a fight for life." *Tampa Bay Times,* January 9, 1984.

Sanders, Jacquin; Keefer, Beirne. "Please god, don't let her drown." *Tampa Bay Times,* January 10, 1984.

Sanders, Jacquin; Keefer, Beirne. "Unsing hero: 'I only knew I could hear this girl crying for help." *Tampa Bay Times,* January 11, 1984.

Sanders, Jacquin; Keefer, Beirne. "The Golden Rule in action, several times over." *Tampa Bay Times,* January 12, 1984.

Sanders, Jacquin; Keefer, Beirne. "The aftermath: For survivors and heroes, life would never be the same." *Tampa Bay Times,* January 13, 1984.

Burgess, John. "Fatal take-off: Survivors tell of terror as jet shuddered." *Washington Post,* March 2, 1982.

Clark, Doug. "Survivor, hero of plane crash recounts ordeal." *The Spokesman-Review,* February 9, 1997.

Schudel, Matt. "Gene Windsor, 74; aided in dramatic plane crash rescue." *Boston Globe,* Septeber 6, 2014.

Battiata, Mary; Koncius, Jura. "A survivor: '. . . we weren't going to make it.'" *Washington Post*, January 14, 1982.

Garry, Candace. "U.S. Park Police – heroes over the Potomac." *Courier: The National Park Service Newsletter*, February 1982.

Henry, Chris. "Rescue over the Potomac." Experimental Aircraft Association News, May 19, 2016. https://www.eaa.org/eaa/news-and-publications/eaa-news-and-aviation-news/news/05-19-2016-rescue-over-the-potomac. Accessed February 24, 2025.

"Rescuers brave icy waters to pull victims from Potomac." *Bangor Daily News*, January 14, 1982.

Cullen, Robert. "'Witnesses say airliner 'too low.'" *Owensboro Messenger-Inquirer*, January 14, 1982.

Witness to History – Eagle One: Rescue and Recovery of Air Florida Flight 90. National Law Enforcement Museum, Washington, DC, January 31, 2017. https://youtu.be/Q_z2lhIUEco. Accessed February 24, 2025.

Augenstein, Neal. "40 years ago on WTOP: Air Florida crash, fatal Metro derailment, snowstorm." WTOP News, January 13, 2022. https://wtop.com/local/2022/01/40-years-ago-on-wtop-air-florida-crash-fatal-metro-derailment-snowstorm. Accessed February 24, 2025.

Statter, Dave. "30 years ago today, twin disasters in DC." STATter911, January 13, 2012. https://statter911.com/2012/01/13/30-years-ago-today-twin-disasters-in-dc-air-florida-flight-90-crashes-into-the-potomac-river-followed-by-the-first-fatal-metro-train-accident-dcfd-radio-traffic-lessons-learned-more. Accessed February 24, 2025.

Statter, Dave. "A look back at another river crash." STATter911, January 16, 2009. https://statter911.com/2009/01/16/a-look-back-to-another-river-crash-air-florida-flight-90-in-dc-had-a-significant-impact-on-regional-cooperation-and-crew-resource-management. Accessed February 24, 2025.

Rich, Cindy. "Pre-internet journalism." *Washingtonian*, January 5, 2012. https://www.washingtonian.com/2012/01/05/pre-internet-citizen-journalism. Accessed February 24, 2025.

"3 studies of capital subway crash begin." *New York Times*, January 15, 1982.

"Investigation teams begin to untangle mystery of Washington subway crash." *Tampa Tribune*, January 15, 1982.

Komarow, Steven. "Three probes begin into subway crash." *Lexington Herald*, January 15, 1982.

"Experts to investigate crash in DC subway." *Times-News*, January 15, 1982.

"'Wrong switch' kills 3." *Indianapolis News*, January 14, 1982.

Lynton, Stephen J. "Supervisor failed to inspect metro train's wheels." *Washington Post*, January 20, 1982.

Hail, Gerald F. " Safety unit says Metro management shared blame for fatal derailment." *Washington Post*, July 30, 1982.

Burgess, John; Bredemeier, Kenneth. "Derailment probe finds dangerous errors by Metro employees." *Washington Post*, February 26, 1982.

"Minor mishap turns into tragedy when subway is backed into divider." *News-Messenger*, January 14, 1982.

Lynton, Stephen J.; Vesey, Tom. "Metro train derails; 3 die." *Washington Post*, January 14, 1982.

Lynton, Stephen J. "Subway probers focus on supervisor's acts." *Washington Post*, January 16, 1982.

Lynton, Stephen J.; Vesey, Tom. "Human error cited in subway crash." *Washington Post*, January 14, 1982.

"Five victims and their families." *Washington Post*, January 13, 1982.

"3 killed, 23 hurt in DC as subway train derails." *Des Moines Register*, January 14, 1982.

"Subway crash kills 3." *Bangor Daily News*, January 14, 1982

"Excerpts of conversation over Metro derailment." *Washington Post*, February 26, 1982.

Kamen, Al. "Metro to pay $1.5 million." *Washington Post*, March 15, 1982.

Ruehl, Peter. "The scene among Metro passengers was panic." *Baltimore Evening Sun*, January 14, 1982.

Stiley, Felch, and Tirado – Oral History Interview US Park Police Pilot Don Usher. National Law Enforcement Museum, Washington, DC, January 31, 2017. https://youtu.be/m6rqMnmxikU. Accessed February 24, 2025.

Del Guidice, Vinny. "Days of disaster – 1949 & 1982." *Arlington Fire Journal*, February 11, 2005. https://arlingtonfirejournal.blogspot.com/2005/02/days-of-disaster-1949-1982.html. Accessed February 24, 2025.

Hiatt, Fred; Kurtz, Howie. "Emergency services reacted quickly to jetliner's crash." *Washington Post*, January 15, 1982.

Koncius, Jura. "The first stop after disaster." *Washington Post*, January 21, 1982.

Bennett, Susan. "With pen and pad and pluck." *Philadelphia Daily News*, January 14, 1982.

Bennett, Susan. "Tragedy shatters a winter scene's stillness." *Philadelphia Daily News*, January 14, 1982.

Earley, Pete. "'Go Teams' swing into action for tragedy." *Washington Post*, January 14, 1982.

"Washington crash survivors still suffer." *Charlotte Observer*, July 15, 1982.

Hebert, H. Josef. "NTSB's 'Go Team' ready to investigate accidents." *Mount Carmel Daily Republican-Register*, February 5, 1982.

"Divers seek bodies, clues." *Detroit Free Press*, January 15, 1982.

"Five known air crash survivors out of danger doctor reports." *Fort Lauderdale News*, January 14, 1982.

Bredemeier, Kenneth. "$50 million paid in Air Florida crash claims." *Washington Post*, November 25, 1983.

Killam, Betsy. "Pace woman's sister survives airplane crash." *Pensacola News*, January 14, 1982.

"Pinewood, SC, native among victims on bridge." *Charlotte Observer*, January 16, 1982

Bruske, Ed; Barker, Karlyn. "Ex-hostages' big day: Andrews to White House to Crystal City." *Washington Post*, January 27, 1981.

Gutman, Roy. "For the witnesses and rescuers, a gruesome and tragic scene." *Newsday*, January 14, 1982.

Berke, Richard. "Relatives' vigil grim scene." *Baltimore Evening Sun*, January 14, 1982.

Matthews, Curt; Timberg, Robert. "Friends, relatives keep sad vigil near site." *Baltimore Sun*, January 14, 1982.

Tracy, Dan; Goudreau, Rosemary. "Until facts were in, there was hope." *Orlando Sentinel*, January 14, 1982.

Podesta, Jane. "The families' funereal wait for death list." *Newsday*, January 14, 1982.

Kessner, Lawrence. "By the river, a grisly scene of horror." *Baltimore Evening Sun*, January 14, 1982.

PART FOUR

"Attempt to lift tail section fails; 30 bodies recovered." *Tampa Tribune*, January 17, 1982.

"Ice, snow stall grim search." *Tampa Tribune*, January 15, 1982.

Dixon, Douglas S. "Air crash on the Potomac: Medical examiner's view." In R. Adams Cowley (Ed.), *Proceedings: First International Assembly on Emergency Medical Services*, Baltimore MD, June 13–17, 1982.

Smith, Timothy. "2 survivors detail how crash changed their lives." *Seattle Times*, January 12, 2012. https://www.seattletimes.com/nation-world/2 -survivors-detail-how-crash-changed-their-lives. Accessed February 24, 2025.

DeAtley, Craig. "One hundred fifty minutes." *JEMS*, March 1982.

Karr, Albert. "DC crash: The search for clues." *Miami News*, March 4, 1982.

Shaw Jr., Robert D. "Divers find bodies, but no answers." *Miami Herald*, January 17, 1982.

Orrick, Bentley. "Flight 90 – It began as any other flight . . ." *Tampa Tribune*, January 17, 1982.

Hiatt, Fred; Kurtz, Howie. "Victim's lifeline: park police helicopter 'Eagle One'." *Washington Post*, January 14, 1982.

Ripley, Amanda. *The Unthinkable: Who Survives When Disaster Strikes — and Why.* Harmony, 2024.

"Families stand by in shock." *Philadelphia Daily News*, January 14, 1982.

"76 feared dead in D.C. crash." *Philadelphia Daily News*, January 14, 1982.

McQueen, Michael; Battiata, Mary. "Views from the bridge – and of it on TV." *Washington Post*, January 16, 1982.

Stublen, Nash. "5 MacDill soldiers may be among air crash casualties." *Tampa Tribune*, January 15, 1982.

Newman, Bud. "Air Florida crash survivor flies Delta home to Miami." *Miami News*, January 19, 1982.

Kennedy, Jim. "Business trip ends in tragedy; firm loses 7." *Tampa Tribune*, January 15, 1982.

Meyer, Eugene L. "Shattered lives: Kin bury plane crash victim." *Washington Post*, January 22, 1982.

Douglas, Frank. "Prudence, spectators both said 'wait,' but survivors couldn't." *Richmond Times-Dispatch*, April 30, 1989.

Perl, Peter. "A fatal day: How 3 Metro victims fretted about snow, rode train to death." *Washington Post*, January 21, 1982.

Morlin, Bill. "Crash altered survivor's life forever." *Spokane Spokesman Review*, January 15, 1992.

Lyton, Stephen J; Vesey, Tom. "Human error cited in subway crash." *Washington Post*, January 15, 1982.

Pianin, Eric. "DC subway officials reassess safety factors." *Capital Times*, January 18, 1982.

Sinclair, Molly. "2 suspended for role in Metro crash." *Washington Post*, March 12, 1982.

Burgess, John. "Metro staff urges shift in safety policy." *Washington Post*, May 28, 1982.

Wilber, Del Quentin. "A crash's improbable impact." *Washington Post*, January 12, 2007.

Melvin, Don. "Error in cockpit revolutionized training of pilots." *Orlando Sentinel*, January 12, 2024.

Burgess, John. "Board recommends Metro guidelines: Board says Metro train faced collision danger." *Washington Post*, March 20, 1982.

"Emergency Preparedness in the Washington Metropolitan Area." Hearings before the Senate Subcommittee on Government Efficiency and the District of Columbia, 98th Congress, p 208. Proposed Metropolitan Washington Emergency Response Action Plan, Metropolitan Washington Council of Governments.

McAden, Fitz. "Flight 90 took off with snow on wing, worker testifies." *Miami Herald*, March 7, 1982.

Brown, Chip. "Wreckage of sunken jetliner yields its last body." *Washington Post*, January 24, 1982.

"Crash victim pours out heart to First Lady." *Miami Herald*, January 16, 1982.